THE PEOPLE OF THE WAY

THE PEOPLE OF THE WAY

The Story Behind the New Testament

ANTHONY E. GILLES

Nihil Obstat:	Rev. Hilarion Kistner, O.F.M.
	Rev. John J. Jennings
Imprimi Potest:	Rev. Jeremy Harrington, O.F.M.
	Provincial
Imprimatur:	Rev. John L. Cavanaugh, V.G.
	Archdiocese of Cincinnati
	June 4, 1984

The *nihil obstat* and *imprimatur* are a declaration that a book or pamphlet is considered to be free from doctrinal or moral error. It is not implied that those who have granted the *nihil obstat* and *imprimatur* agree with the contents, opinions or statements expressed.

Book design and cover by Julie Lonneman.

SBN 0-86716-036-5

TO ANDREA:
WIFE, FRIEND,
EDITOR-IN-CHIEF

Contents

INTRODUCTION 1

TABLE OF SCRIPTURE ABBREVIATIONS 7

NEW TESTAMENT DEVELOPMENT—A CHART 8

1. THE WITNESS OF THE ACTS COMMUNITY 11
   Acts of the Apostles
   Acts and the Primitive Kerygma 14
   Sources of the New Testament 15
   Luke's Message in Acts 16
   The Heroes of Acts 17
   The Evangelizing Community 18
   From Infatuation to Intimacy 19

2. THE WITNESS OF THE SYNOPTIC GOSPELS 21
   Matthew, Mark, Luke
   The Making of a Gospel 23
   How the Synoptic Gospels Developed 24
   The Personality of Each Gospel 26
   Growing Toward Intimacy With Jesus 31

3. APOSTLE TO THE GENTILES 37
   1 and 2 Thessalonians, 1 and 2 Corinthians
   Paul—Before and After 39
   Paul's Writing 40
   Paul's Focus on the Body 45
   Different Approaches, Same Challenge 47

4. JUSTIFICATION BY FAITH IN JESUS CHRIST 49
   Philippians, Galatians
   How Does One Become Free? 51
   'Justice,' 'Faith' and 'Law' 55

5. 'THE GLORIOUS FREEDOM OF THE CHILDREN OF GOD'   59
   Romans
   Paul's Gospel   60
   Paul's Key Words   61
   Effects of Justification   63
   Responsibilities of Christian Freedom   66

6. LIVING THE NEW WAY   69
   1 and 2 Timothy, Titus, James, 1 and 2 Peter, Jude, Philemon
   Charismatic vs. Institutional?   70
   The Pastoral Letters   71
   Other Letter Writers   73
   A Final Word From Paul   78
   On to the Third Stage   78

7. 'THE MYSTERY OF CHRIST IN YOU'   81
   Colossians, Ephesians
   Paul the Spiritual Master   82
   Who Wrote Colossians?   83
   The Message of Colossians   84
   Who Wrote Ephesians?   86
   The Message of Ephesians   88

8. MEDIATOR OF A NEW COVENANT   91
   Hebrews
   The Platonism in Hebrews   92
   Hebrew's Unique Themes   93
   Hebrews as a Third-Stage Work   94
   The Structure of Hebrews   96

9. 'THE FATHER AND I ARE ONE'   101
    John's Gospel, 1, 2 and 3 John
    The Question of Authorship   102
    John's Abstract Language   103
    Jesus' Discourses   104
    Overview of John's Gospel   106
    1 John   114
    2 and 3 John   116

10. 'SEE, I MAKE ALL THINGS NEW'   117
    Revelation
    Historical and Universal   118
    Revelation, Apocalyptic and the Old Testament   120
    A Key to the Symbols   122
    Revelation as Liturgical Drama   123

CONCLUSION   131
    Christianity: A Spectator Sport   131
    A Human Jesus, a Human Bible   132
    A People of 'the Way'   133

SCRIPTURE INDEX   134

TOPICAL INDEX   138

INTRODUCTION

As we begin a study of the New Testament, we must keep in mind the fundamental constituent of the Jewish faith—the belief that God's revelation to humanity is to be found in the written words of Sacred Scripture. The first Christians preserved this essential ingredient of Judaism as they began to proclaim the Good News of Jesus Christ and to write down for others what they proclaimed. This book is the story of how those first Christians moved from proclamation to writing—and thus how they gave us the New Testament.*

The New Testament—like its predecessor, the Old Testament—evolved out of the shared experiences of a particular group of people. Just as the Old Testament came into existence within the context of Israelite history, so the New Testament came into existence within the context of the communal life of the first Christians. This leads to our basic premise: *The early Church formed the New Testament; the New Testament did not form the early Church.*

Some Christians today look upon the New Testament as if the first Christians waited until it was composed before they dared take any organized action to spread the gospel. In reality, a body of believers was already proclaiming the gospel before any written document appeared.

---

*The story of how the Jews got their sacred books in the first place—the story behind the Old Testament—is covered in my first volume, *The People of the Book,* also from St. Anthony Messenger Press.

1

As a result, we cannot go back to "pure Bible Christianity"—as some people put it—because Christianity did not come into existence in response to a book. The first Christians responded to a person. It was only after a period of shared reflection on their relationship with that person that they composed what we call the New Testament.

We will find, then, that New Testament authors had their own purposes for writing. And we must understand these purposes from *their* point of view if we are to understand the books they wrote. We cannot impose on their writings our preconceived, 20th-century ideas about what they were trying to say.

THE PERSON BEHIND THE NEW TESTAMENT

What motivated the first Christians to write the words of the New Testament? We must first answer a more basic question: What motivated the first Christians to *proclaim* the Good News of Jesus Christ?

From within the depths of the confusion and turmoil which characterized first-century Palestine, people were suddenly inspired to proclaim that Jesus of Nazareth was Messiah and Lord. Something dramatic, durable and revolutionary occurred in their lives. They became transformed—some would later say they had become new creations: "...if anyone is in Christ, he is a new creation" (2 Corinthians 5:17).

Any attempt to understand why the New Testament was written must take into account this initial earthshaking revolution in human consciousness on the part of the first believers. Because of their change in consciousness—their *metanoia*, to use the Greek word—the first Christians could not but tell others of their new lives in Christ. This testimony of their own experience of Jesus the Lord formed the basis of their proclamations, and it was that same testimony which they incorporated into their first writings about Jesus.

As to their purpose in *writing*, we can point to several factors: First, there was the ordinary human desire to preserve an important tradition before it was forgotten. Second, as more and more people became interested in joining the body of believers, the need increased for a common set of written teachings about Jesus.

But the *primary purpose* of the first Christian writers was to lead others to know Jesus in the same way they themselves knew him. So the substance of their writings was not so much a set of facts or a dogma—but a person. They hoped, in their writing, to bring others into relationship with that person: Jesus Christ.

Thus we cannot understand the New Testament unless we approach it, on the one hand, as a book about Jesus and, on the other,

2

as a book about the early Christians' developing relationship with Jesus. For that reason we will try in the pages ahead to identify with these first-century believers as they initially became attracted to the person of Jesus and as they gradually deepened their relationship with him.

As we do so, we will discover that the formation of the New Testament is really a subplot within the central "love story" of the first believers' developing relationship with Jesus. This book will attempt to relate various types of New Testament writing to the stages in this developing "love relationship."

We shall see, then, how the New Testament developed part and parcel with the growth in faith of the first Christians. This is the exciting aspect of our story—the story *behind* the New Testament.

We will begin this story by asking that fundamental question which stirred the first believers: "Who is Jesus of Nazareth?" We will discover the various contexts in which the first seekers asked that question as well as the various contexts in which the early Church—the body of believers—answered it.

As those first believers found their answers to that fundamental question, those very answers led them to ask still deeper questions about Jesus. So will we likewise move on to consider the New Testament books which answer those deeper questions. Thus we will parallel the stages of the early believers' growth of faith in Jesus Christ with stages of New Testament writing and development.

Paul himself commented on the "stages" found in early Christian experience:

> Brothers, the trouble was that I could not talk to you as spiritual men but only as men of flesh, as infants in Christ. I fed you with milk, and did not give you solid food because you were not ready for it.
> (1 Corinthians 3:1-2)

STAGE ONE: INFATUATION

What was it that first prompted a significant number of people to ask, "Who is Jesus of Nazareth?"

We know from the Gospels that many people sought after Jesus and that he greatly influenced the lives of many people while he was still alive. Yet, in reality, Jesus' mission was something of a failure until after his death. On the day of his crucifixion everyone had deserted him except several loyal women and one man (see John 19:25-26).

There were few people on Calvary who saw in Jesus' sagging and tortured body their Savior and their Lord. The public that day was

3

confronted with the spectacle of a defeated criminal, not a triumphant Lord.

It was only because of Jesus' resurrection and its proclamation by the first believers that we came to have the four Gospels and the other New Testament writings. Without that *first stage—that confrontation by the first believers with the risen Lord of glory*—nothing else would have taken place. Since Acts of the Apostles is the New Testament book which depicts how the early body of believers first became convinced of Jesus' lordship, and how they proclaimed their conviction to others, we start with Acts in the pages ahead.

What happened in the relationship between Jesus and the first Christians is very similar to what occurs in any love relationship. First, the early Christians "fell in love" with the risen Jesus, the Lord of Glory. Everyone in town could tell they were head over heels in love just by looking at their faces. And, like anyone in love, they proclaimed to everyone both the fact of their infatuation and the many good points about their beloved. The twin themes of this first stage of New Testament development, then, are *infatuation* and *proclamation*.

STAGE TWO: INTIMACY

The second stage in New Testament development, the stage of *intimacy*, has its parallel in an ordinary love relationship too. This is the stage where lovers seek to find out all they can about the beloved. They exchange lengthy letters, take long walks and otherwise get to know each other. It is this maturing intimacy between the first Christians and their Lord which characterizes the second stage of New Testament development.

Once the early Church had come to know that Jesus was Messiah and Lord, the next thing it wanted to know was more detailed information about him. The Gospels of Matthew, Mark and Luke—the first set of books we will consider in this second stage—answer questions which any new lover of Jesus would naturally have asked: Where was Jesus born? Where did he grow up? What kinds of things did he say and do? (As we shall see in Chapter Two, these Gospels are not biographies and address themselves to deeper questions than vital statistics about Jesus. Yet one impulse behind their writing was this natural curiosity to know more about Jesus.)

Other books of this second stage of New Testament development are 1 and 2 Thessalonians, 1 and 2 Timothy, Titus, 1 and 2 Corinthians, Galatians, Romans, Philippians, Philemon, James, 1 and 2 Peter and Jude. These writings accomplish many of the same things as Matthew,

4

Mark and Luke, but in different ways. For example, while the Gospels certainly emphasize the implementation of Jesus' teachings in one's daily life, these other writings focus more specifically on *how*.

For instance, the evangelist Luke has Jesus saying, "Whoever wishes to be my follower must deny his very self, take up his cross each day, and follow in my steps" (9:23). Luke gives many examples of how Jesus denied his very self as he moved toward the cross. Yet a disciple living 30 or so years after Jesus' death would find many new situations in which to ask, "How do I apply Jesus' teaching on denying myself to *this* situation?"

It was one thing for the early Christians to fall in love with Jesus. It was another thing to know him more intimately and to adopt his values and put them into practice in their own lives. It is precisely at this point that many lovers separate. They are not willing to pay the price of surrendering some of their own needs and desires in order to accept the values of their beloved.

The writers of the second stage—the stage of intimacy—were trying to get the first believers to move beyond infatuation to an intimate relationship with Jesus. Yet there is still a third stage, an even deeper level of relationship with the Lord. At this level the believer is not only intimate with the Lord but becomes *identified* with him.

STAGE THREE: IDENTIFICATION

Writers in the third stage of New Testament development—the stage of *identification* with Jesus—have advanced well beyond infatuation and intimacy. Such a profound knowledge of the Lord is expressed in this stage that we sense the authors were at times writing from within Jesus' own consciousness.

This third stage in New Testament development likewise parallels a love relationship. After the exuberance of infatuation, after getting to know one's lover more intimately and surrendering many personal desires in order to share the values of the beloved, lovers become so united as to share virtually the same identity. We see this in mature married couples who have lived together so long that they even begin to look alike. Such couples know each other so well—they are so like-minded—that they practically share the same consciousness.

Two separate sets of books make up this third stage: first of all, Ephesians, Colossians and Hebrews; second, the Gospel of John, the Johannine epistles and the Book of Revelation. (Revelation really defies categorization with any other New Testament work. For our purposes, however, we will consider it along with the writings associated with the apostle John, giving it special treatment as we do so.)

Let us begin our journey now through the stages of New Testament development by taking up the story of the early Church's developing love affair with Jesus.

TABLE OF SCRIPTURE ABBREVIATIONS

Acts—Acts of the Apostles
Am—Amos
Bar—Baruch
1 Chr—1 Chronicles
2 Chr—2 Chronicles
Col—Colossians
1 Cor—1 Corinthians
2 Cor—2 Corinthians
Dn—Daniel
Dt—Deuteronomy
Eccl—Ecclesiastes
Eph—Ephesians
Est—Esther
Ex—Exodus
Ez—Ezekiel
Ezr—Ezra
Gal—Galatians
Gn—Genesis
Hb—Habakkuk
Heb—Hebrews
Hg—Haggai
Hos—Hosea
Is—Isaiah
Jas—James
Jb—Job
Jdt—Judith
Jer—Jeremiah
Jl—Joel
Jgs—Judges
Jn—John
1 Jn—1 John
2 Jn—2 John
3 Jn—3 John
Jon—Jonah
Jos—Joshua
Jude—Jude
1 Kgs—1 Kings
2 Kgs—2 Kings
Lam—Lamentations
Lk—Luke
Lv— Leviticus
Mal—Malachi
1 Mc—1 Maccabees
2 Mc—2 Maccabees
Mi—Micah

Mk—Mark
Mt—Matthew
Na—Nahum
Neh—Nehemiah
Nm—Numbers
Ob—Obadiah
1 Pt—1 Peter
2 Pt—2 Peter
Phil—Philippians
Phlm—Philemon
Prv—Proverbs
Ps—Psalms
Rom—Romans
Ru—Ruth
Rv—Revelation
Song—Song of Songs
Sir—Ecclesiasticus (Sirach)
1 Sm—1 Samuel
2 Sm—2 Samuel
Tb— Tobit
1 Thes—1 Thessalonians
2 Thes—2 Thessalonians
Ti—Titus
1 Tm—1 Timothy
2 Tm—2 Timothy
Wis—Wisdom
Zec—Zechariah
Zep—Zephaniah

NEW TESTAMENT DEVELOPMENT

	Work
Stage One (Infatuation)	Acts of the Apostles
Stage Two (Intimacy)	Matthew Mark Luke 1 Thessalonians 2 Thessalonians 1, 2 Corinthians Philippians Galatians Romans 1, 2 Timothy Titus James 1, 2 Peter Jude Philemon
Stage Three (Identification)	Colossians Ephesians Hebrews Gospel of John 1, 2, 3 John
Epilogue (A Christian theology of history)	Revelation

Author	Date
The evangelist Luke	80-85 A.D.

The School of Matthew	70-80
The evangelist Mark	64-70
The evangelist Luke	80-85
Paul the Apostle	51
Anonymous	80-90
Paul the Apostle	56-57
Paul the Apostle	56
Paul the Apostle	54
Paul the Apostle	58
Anonymous	80-90
Anonymous	80-90
Anonymous	80-90
Anonymous	80-90
Anonymous	80-90
Paul the Apostle	61-63

Paul the Apostle	61-63
Paul the Apostle (parts of)	61-63
(Perhaps) Apollos of Alexandria	80-90
John the Apostle and his school	90-95
John the Apostle and his school	90-95

John of Ephesus	90-95

9

CHAPTER ONE

THE WITNESS OF THE ACTS COMMUNITY

Acts of the Apostles

Let us imagine that you are a pious Jew living in Jerusalem in the year 35 A.D. As you enter into this time and culture, pretend that you are the same sex, age and economic status as the "20th-century you."

You share with your fellow first-century Jews certain historical experiences that make your people unique. In this uniqueness you find a certain bond uniting you so firmly with your brothers and sisters that differences of age, sex or occupation cannot separate you.

To begin with, you believe very strongly that you are a member of a "chosen people"—a people set apart centuries ago by Yahweh to be made holy. Throughout the many epochs of your people's history, this has frequently meant much suffering as your ancestors resisted Yahweh, refusing to heed his voice and allow him to mold their hearts. Instead, as you know only too well from reading the Scriptures, they were often stiff-necked and arrogant before Yahweh.

Yet Yahweh always raised up righteous ones to turn the people back to their true God. Your Scriptures preserve stories of Isaiah, Jeremiah and Ezekiel—the great prophets; of Ezra, "the lawgiver," and Nehemiah, who five centuries before your time led your ancestors in rebuilding the walls of the fallen Temple and of the devastated city of Jerusalem. And, of course, there are those almost legendary figures who most inspire you today: Tobit, Judith, Esther, Daniel, the Maccabees.

The very names stir your blood and make you proud to be a Jew. Why? Because these figures more than any other teach you how a good Jew is to behave in a pagan environment. And Palestine in your era is most decidedly a land besieged by paganism.

For two centuries, your ancestors have longed fervently for the coming of a liberator to end your oppression by these pagans. The writer of the Book of Daniel had prophesied the coming of "one like a son of man" (7:13). It was said of this mysterious figure that his "dominion...shall not be taken away, his kingship shall not be destroyed" (7:14).

But who was this "one like a son of man?" Many people in your day—rightly or wrongly—have begun to apply this passage on the son of man to the anticipated Messiah—the anointed one, the hoped-for savior. Your grandfather had thought that perhaps Judas Maccabeus was the Messiah. But, alas, the Maccabees' descendants betrayed your people, and the despised Herodians soon came to power.

Some of your friends believe the Messiah is not a man at all. They believe that Yahweh himself will drive the Gentile oppressors from your land. According to them, the "one like a son of man" is really Yahweh's mighty angel who, with a flaming sword, will slaughter Romans and Herodians alike.

Other friends remind you of Yahweh's ancient promise to King David to keep his "royal throne firm forever" (2 Samuel 7:13). These friends tell you, "You will see. Our Messiah will be a king like David. He will even be descended from David." "But how can there be a descendant of David in these times?" you wonder. "The last king descended from David died centuries ago!"

Then there is that strangest of all the beliefs about the Messiah, held by a minority of the rabbis. "The Messiah will have to suffer," old Rabbi Jacob taught you once years ago. "He will be a servant to his people." The old man quoted verses from Isaiah:

> Oppressed and condemned, he was taken away,
> and who would have thought any more of his destiny?
> When he was cut off from the land of the living,
> and smitten for the sin of his people.... (Isaiah 53:8)

It is difficult to know what to believe about the Messiah. When will he come? How will he make his appearance known? Will he slaughter the Romans? "Oh, Yahweh!" you pray. "Send our Messiah to us soon. Drive the oppressors from our land. Restore your kingdom to your servant David, our father!"

These thoughts are on your mind this morning as you come upon a group of Jews standing near the corner of the market square. One of them—a Jew you know—is speaking about the very subject of your thoughts: "This Jesus whom our elders have crucified is the Messiah, the promised savior of our people!"

What amazing things the man says about this Jesus of Nazareth! You are spellbound. Can it really be? You have heard so many different ideas about the Messiah. How can you be sure this man's words are true? When he finishes speaking, you approach him quietly and look into his eyes. You find acceptance, trust, encouragement. You cannot suppress the question that is nearly bursting from your lips: "My friend, who is Jesus of Nazareth?"

"I will tell you about Jesus of Nazareth," he says. "But we cannot talk here. I must return to the Temple in time for afternoon prayer. They are all waiting for me. Won't you join us?"

More out of curiosity than boldness you walk with your friend through the maze-like streets of Jerusalem toward the Temple. You notice that several of your fellow Jews whisper and point in your direction as you walk along.

"Look," one of them hisses, clutching a companion's sleeve, "there is one of the followers of the Nazarean. Why don't the priests simply arrest them all?"

Your friend smiles at you. "Don't let them bother you. I was like them once, until I came to know about the new way."

" 'New way'?" you repeat. "What on earth are you talking about?"

Before your friend can answer, the two of you have reached the gate of the Temple. Silently you enter and proceed to the East Portico. A crowd of perhaps 200 people is gathered. Nothing unusual appears to be happening. The people are reciting a Psalm. A song or two is sung. A passage from the prophet Jeremiah is read.

You feel completely at ease here—this is just like a synagogue service. Then the crowd becomes silent as a middle-aged man stands to address the body. His face is rough and weather-beaten, his hands are leathery. Even before he speaks you guess, "A fisherman! Reminds me of Cousin Benjamin from Galilee." Sure enough, the man has a decidedly northern accent.

"My brothers and sisters!" he begins, waiting for silence to settle over the crowd. "We give praise and thanks to our Father, God most high, for giving us his marvelous blessings today. As you know, last night our brother John and I were arrested again. Once again we were flogged for proclaiming the name of our Lord Jesus. Once again we were released with a warning never to proclaim that name in public again. Yet we are back today, proclaiming even more strongly the signs of these latter days—that God has brought us our Messiah! This Jesus whom our elders crucified, and who rose from the dead on the third

13

day, is Lord. It is by him, and through the power of God's Holy Spirit, that we return to you again today to proclaim salvation for our people Israel, through the forgiveness of sin in Jesus' name. Let all here who have not repented of their sins do so now. Let them accept forgiveness of sins and Baptism in the name of the Lord Jesus, so that the Spirit of God most high may pour out his mighty power upon them!"

You stand dumbfounded as several Jews walk forward. Such incredible words! This Jesus is called "Lord," a name reserved only for Yahweh himself. He is said to have "risen from the dead," and it is "through his name" that "sins are forgiven." You are too shocked to move.

Your friend looks at you and quietly says, "Now you know who Jesus of Nazareth is. Will you accept him? Will you let him be your Messiah?"

"I...I...I don't know. I mean, I don't know what to make of all this," you stammer.

Your friend looks at you and gently takes your hand. "I know, my friend, I know. Come, we will talk some more. I will introduce you to our elders. You will learn more about the new way."

ACTS AND THE PRIMITIVE KERYGMA

Thus begins your introduction to Christianity. In order to find out how the story ends, it is not necessary to continue our imagined dialogue. Instead we may turn to a New Testament book specifically concerned with answering the perplexed Jew's question, "Who is Jesus of Nazareth?" In the Acts of the Apostles we find recorded some of the young Church's first reflections on the person of this Jesus of Nazareth.

That is not to say that Acts was the first New Testament book written. Several of Paul's epistles were written as early as three decades before Acts. Paul's First Letter to the Thessalonians, for example, was written around the year 51, whereas Acts was committed to writing by the evangelist Luke perhaps around the year 85 (see pp. 8-9).

We begin with Acts because we find recorded there the accounts of how the early Church first began to understand and proclaim the person of Jesus. These first accounts are often referred to by scholars as the "primitive kerygma." (The Greek word *kerygma* means "proclamation.")

This primitive kerygma grew spontaneously out of the love affair which the first disciples had with Jesus. As they came to love him they naturally wanted to proclaim him to others, just as someone newly in love wants to tell the world about his or her beloved. The primitive

14

kerygma is thus the core of the *first stage of New Testament development—the stage of infatuation.*

When Luke wrote Acts he had at his disposal a number of sources from this primitive kerygma—such things as oral testimony and prior written accounts of the ministry of Jesus. To this primitive kerygma he may have added his own travel notes from his sojourns with the apostle Paul. Luke needed the help of prior witnesses in writing Acts because he had not himself been an eyewitness to Jesus' ministry.

SOURCES OF THE NEW TESTAMENT

In *The People of the Book*, I discussed the various sources which went into the fabrication of the Old Testament. Much of what I said there applies here, too, although the sources used by the respective Old and New Testament writers were very different, of course.

As with the Old Testament, the writers of the New Testament, such as Luke, were not stenographers—that is, they did not record verbatim everything they saw and heard. Nor were they present at every event or occurrence about which they wrote. They depended on *sources*.

Some people reported orally to the writers on events in Jesus' life which they had seen or heard; others passed on bits and pieces of written information about Jesus which they had in their possession. For our purposes, then, a *source* may be defined simply as preexisting information about Jesus—oral or written—which a New Testament writer used to write his particular book.

Thus when we read the New Testament we are reading a mixture of *original* material and *borrowed* material. A good example of the former is Paul's account of the first years of his apostolate, in Galatians 1:11—2:14. There Paul wrote directly from his own memory of the described events and relied on no preexisting source.

An obvious example of borrowed material is found in 1 Corinthians 15:1-11. Paul was writing to remind the Corinthians of the resurrection appearances of Jesus. In 15:3,6 Paul says, "I handed on to you first of all what I *myself received*,...that *Jesus* was seen by five hundred brothers at once..." (emphasis added). In other words, Paul was not present when Jesus appeared to the 500 brothers. He heard about this later from someone else and passed along the information to others in his First Letter to the Corinthians. In this passage, then, Paul very clearly relied on a preexisting source to relay his message.

It is not always this easy to know which portions of a New Testament writing are original accounts and which depend on source material. Scripture scholars have waged protracted debates over the question, and there is by no means unanimity of opinion among them on this question. In this book we will follow the general consensus among scholars and not get diverted by the fine points of the debate.

LUKE'S MESSAGE IN ACTS

Tradition has it that Luke was a doctor from one of the Greek-speaking cities of Asia Minor. He was probably a teenager when Jesus died. In some way he came to hear about Jesus—we don't know how, why or when. It may have been in Antioch that the Gentile doctor first heard from certain Jews the story of their Messiah—Jesus of Nazareth. However it came about, Luke's conversion to Christianity must have been dramatic and thorough. Imagine a Greek doctor converting to a spiritual movement within Judaism that was regarded by the mainstream of the Jews themselves as heretical!

To put it in a nutshell, Luke tells in the Acts of the Apostles (1) how God the Father, (2) through the Holy Spirit, (3) spread the Good News of Jesus Christ (4) from Jerusalem to the far reaches of the known world. Let's analyze that statement.

Who?

God the Father, Luke emphasizes over and over again, is responsible for the action described in Acts. Christianity is unstoppable because it is God's will that it be spread.

How?

God facilitates this through the power of the Holy Spirit. Thus Acts has frequently been called "the Gospel of the Holy Spirit." In Acts we discover how Jesus' words—"It is much better for you that I go" (John 16:7)—are fulfilled. We find that Jesus' gift of the Holy Spirit becomes the means the Father uses to empower Jesus' followers to proclaim the gospel and unify the first believers.

What?

Jesus Christ is the Good News proclaimed in Acts. It is Jesus who has freed humanity from the bondage of sin. It is Jesus who is the means of salvation. Jesus, thus, is the focal point of the teaching in Acts.

Where?

From Jerusalem to Rome and, by implication, throughout the known world—that is where the Good News of Jesus is preached. Acts is the story of how the Good News of Jesus is offered first to the Jews,

16

beginning in Jerusalem, and then to the Gentiles.

THE HEROES OF ACTS

The two principal heroes of Luke's story are Peter and Paul. Both men learn that God's intention is to include all people in his plan of salvation; they both become spokesmen for the proclamation of the Good News to the Gentiles. Generally speaking, the first half of Acts focuses on Peter's activities, the second half on Paul's.

We could say in summary that in Acts we see how the earliest Christians became infatuated with Jesus and how they proclaimed their infatuation to others. We thus observe the unfolding of the first stage of New Testament development.

Luke begins Acts in the same way he begins his Gospel—by stressing the role of the Holy Spirit. Just as the Holy Spirit was the moving force behind Jesus' conception (Luke 1:35), so likewise is the Spirit the moving force behind the birth of the young Church. After Jesus' ascension into heaven (Acts 1), the little flock of disciples gathers in Jerusalem. On the day of Pentecost they are suddenly surprised by the Holy Spirit (Acts 2).

The transforming power of the Spirit's work is immediately evident. We find that the very disciple who three times had denied Jesus suddenly becomes the boldest public spokesman among the apostles on behalf of Jesus. The Spirit has transformed Peter's former impetuosity into genuine forthrightness and courage.

After Luke's account of the descent of the Holy Spirit, he begins his teaching on the person of Jesus in the form of speeches by various disciples. The first speech is Peter's (Acts 2:14-41).

In this discourse Peter teaches the person of Jesus as Messiah and Lord. Peter first makes the point (2:23-32) that although Jesus gave convincing evidence he was God's Son, he was rejected. Despite this, Peter continues, Jesus overcame sin and death and is exalted forever in his risen glory. To this same Jesus the disciples bear witness.

Now comes the difficult part (2:36-37). By laying the blame for the denial of Jesus' lordship directly on "the whole house of Israel," Peter dramatically brings his audience to a moment of personal decision-making. *"You* crucified" this Jesus, Peter proclaims. The reason for Luke's use of discourse is now evident. Every hearer of the Word must now ask, "What must *I* do?"

The answer which Peter gives highlights the fundamental Christian message stressed repeatedly in Acts: (1) Repent and (2) be baptized, so that (3) your sins are forgiven and (4) you can receive the

Holy Spirit. The gift of the Holy Spirit will empower the new Christian to serve as a witness to Jesus, following in the footsteps of Peter and the other evangelists.

THE EVANGELIZING COMMUNITY

It is evident as we proceed through Acts that Peter and his fellow evangelists envisage the formation of a body of witnesses, co-evangelists who will spread the gospel to the four corners of the world. Through Peter and John, Philip, Stephen and especially Paul, Luke shows us how the faith community became an evangelizing community. This group of Jesus' followers—being comprised mostly of Jews—first proclaimed the Good News to other Jews. It is when the community begins to take the message of Jesus to Gentiles that the story really becomes intriguing.

Luke begins his account of the conversion of the Gentiles with the conversion of the Roman centurion, Cornelius, and his baptism by Peter (Acts 10). With this foundation laid, Luke takes up the story of the Gentiles' conversion on a large scale. The starting point for this movement is Antioch.

Christian inroads into the Antioch community were made, not by the apostles or other more noteworthy evangelists, but simply by "some men of Cyprus and Cyrene" (11:20). The young Church's first full-scale evangelization effort was thus undertaken not by the "hierarchy" but by the "laity"! Notice that it is only after news of the Gentile conversions in Antioch "reached the ears" of the apostles (11:22) that Barnabas is sent to authenticate these conversions.

Prior to the time of the Antioch conversions, Jewish converts to Christianity had been generally known as "Nazarenes" rather than "Christians." *Christian* is derived from *Christos*, the Greek word for Messiah, "anointed one." Belief in the coming of a Messiah was common among Jews; only for Gentiles would belief in a *Christos* be so significant as to justify being named for such a belief. That is why "it was in Antioch that the disciples were called Christians for the first time" (11:26b).

The first Gentile converts had been integrated into the Jewish milieu in which the first Christian evangelists lived. In Acts 13:44-52 we find a new development. The Jewish audiences of Paul and Barnabas reject the Good News, thus opening the way for the start of separate Gentile Churches outside of the Jewish religious and cultural environment.

We find events such as those depicted in Acts 13 repeated often by Luke. They form something of a pattern for Paul's activities throughout the remainder of Acts: The gospel is taken to the Jews, who reject it, necessitating its being preached to the Gentiles, who accept it. What occurs in the process is that certain communities in the young Church slowly slip away from their Jewish moorings and begin to set sail as uniquely Gentile-Christian bodies.

Luke weaves his account of the Church's mission to the Gentiles around his story of the career of Paul. Since we will read more about Paul in upcoming chapters, suffice it to say here that after an evangelistic career involving much hardship and turmoil, Paul makes it to Rome. Following the typical pattern throughout Acts, Paul—ever the missionary—first approaches the local Jews with the message of salvation. As elsewhere, many Jews reject the gospel (28:24), and we surmise that Paul then proclaims the gospel to Roman Gentiles (28:30).

Luke ends Acts at this point in Paul's ministry. There is a tradition which places Luke in Rome with Paul during the "two full years" of Paul's stay.

FROM INFATUATION TO INTIMACY

Acts, then, begins and ends focusing on the early Church's proclamation of Jesus as Messiah and Lord. This first stage of New Testament development reflects the early Christians' infatuation with the person of Jesus and their enthusiasm about proclaiming his gospel. Anyone listening to the testimony of the Acts evangelists would have said to themselves, "Perhaps I had better learn *more* about this Jesus whom these Christians proclaim."

We will now turn to the writers of the second stage of New Testament development who address themselves to this need for more knowledge about Jesus. Just as lovers go through a phase of infatuation and then want to grow closer by learning everything about each other, so too the early Christians wanted to grow in *intimacy* with Christ by finding out more details of his life and teachings. New Testament authors provide this information in two different ways—through the Gospels of Matthew, Mark and Luke, and through certain letters of Paul and other New Testament letter writers.

CHAPTER TWO

THE WITNESS OF THE SYNOPTIC GOSPELS

Matthew, Mark, Luke

The old woman pushed aside the first basket of clothes she had washed that morning and prepared to beat a second soggy heap on the smooth rocks. Down the shore she saw her neighbor with his fishing crew, making his way toward the lake in his usual style—arms swinging, shouting orders at high pitch to the other men. He turned and spotted her.

"You'll wait up for me tonight, won't you, Grandmother?" he yelled. His conceited grin beamed at her down the water. "We'll hug under the full moon," he said, caressing his beard with a mocking look of passion on his face.

"Not unless you wash that stench off your carcass first, fisherman! Hug those fellows—they're more your style!"

He and his mates groaned and whistled, then stamped off, leaving her to her chores. Around the cove, through the palm trees, she could see his boat resting at anchor, as untidy and rough as its owner. She liked the fisherman—everyone in the village did. He had an exuberance about him that drew people to him—even if his manner was somewhat abrasive.

The man had been left an adequate little fishing boat by his father, along with well-mended nets which had borne the tests of many years of fishing in the briny waters. He did not make much—just enough to feed his mother-in-law and younger brother, and now and then to buy some supplies for the family fig orchard.

The younger brother had a streak of impracticality which greatly annoyed the man. In his younger days there had been neither time nor

21

money available to dabble in the latest popular causes—or in "prophet-chasing," as he described his younger brother's most recent interest. Every week, it seemed, some new teacher passed through the village making grandiose proclamations, drawing the young men away from their work in the process.

On the way to the boat that morning, the fisherman decided that today would be a good time to suggest to his younger brother that he was wasting his time with these "prophets," especially now that the boy and his friends had apparently settled on one they wanted to follow in earnest.

"I noticed you got in late again last night," the man began. "You weren't wasting time with your friend 'the prophet,' were you?"

"I didn't consider it a waste of time," his brother replied. "Besides, I've made no secret about where I've been going, and I've always invited you along."

"I've got work to do, remember?" the man responded. "And it might not be a bad idea for *you* to be a bit more diligent these days."

"What have I neglected? I get my work done. Look, couldn't you come, just once? I know what you think, but this man is different. If you could hear him speak you would know what I mean. I think he's like *you* in some ways. Please come—today. We're all to meet him this afternoon."

"Like *me*, is he! Then bring him here with you, and I'll put a net in his hands!"

"He *is* like you. Do you find it so hard to think that I might use good judgment in choosing my associates?"

The man sighed. "I suppose there's nothing I can do but let you learn the hard way."

"Then you mean you'll come and meet him?" the younger man asked hopefully.

"I didn't say *that*! I'll think it over. *You* can go—this afternoon, anyway."

After lunch the younger brother went to meet his friends. The older brother remained behind to mend the nets. Toward sunset, earlier than either of them had expected, the younger man returned.

From a hill above the shore, where the old washwoman often sat to catch the evening breeze, she saw the two brothers sitting quietly on the sand, knees at chin level, looking intently at each other as they talked. Soon a man came around the base of the hill into the woman's line of vision—a stranger. There was nothing about him out of the ordinary. A half dozen other men were with him, and she recognized one or two.

22

The younger brother went out to greet the stranger, bringing his older brother to the man's side and introducing them. To the old woman the fisherman seemed locked to the spot. He moved not a muscle, but stared fixedly at the stranger while the latter spoke. In a few minutes the stranger went back down the shore with his companions. The brothers followed—slowly and well behind at first, then faster, until they caught up with the rest.

The woman rarely saw the two brothers after that day. Someone told her they went off with the stranger, traveling from town to town with him on some sort of "mission" he had to accomplish.

One day, months later, she saw the brothers coming up the hill toward the village accompanied by strangers—Greeks, she thought, judging from their clothes and speech. She noticed that one of the men called the older brother by a new name. "*Petros*," she whispered. "What an odd name!"

The Making of a Gospel

Imagine for a moment that you are the old washwoman described above. Imagine further that you soon discover who the "stranger" on the shore really was—Jesus of Nazareth, a man acclaimed by many of your fellow Jews to be the Messiah. You hear that he was crucified in Jerusalem and, as one itinerant preacher proclaimed, that he was raised by God from the dead. Attracted by such declarations, you seek out the small band of people in your village who call themselves followers of Jesus.

They share with you their stories and remembrances of the two brothers from your village who accompanied Jesus in his ministry. One evening you timidly start to describe the incident you witnessed on the lakeshore and—to your surprise—your listeners seem fascinated. One man says, "Imagine that! Right here in our village!" A woman in the party says, "We'll have to remember that—it's too good to forget. I always wondered how those two fellows met the Christ!" The story circulates among the villagers and is told over and over again.

You, the washwoman, now qualify to be called one of the first Christian "evangelizers"—or "gospel spreaders." The word *gospel* simply means "good news." By making your small contribution to spreading the Good News of Jesus, you have participated in the larger process of spreading the Good News which will take place throughout Palestine, Syria, Greece, Italy and, eventually, the entire world.

In fact, your little episode in the life of Jesus will even make its way into print. Years later, certain evangelizers will take the process of gospel-spreading one step further by writing down stories like yours in manuscripts which will come to be titled—appropriately—*Gospels*. These Gospel writers will not record your story exactly as you told it, because they will use the story for a purpose you never contemplated. Nevertheless, they will put your contribution to the "gospel of Jesus Christ" to good use. (See, for example, how "your story" appears in Matthew 4:18-20.)

This imaginary account of how one passage in the Gospels came to be written may not—for all we know—be far wrong. To gain a proper understanding of the Gospels and what they mean, we must keep in mind that many oral gospels like the one above went into the making of the final written Gospels.

Matthew, like the other Gospel writers, did not sit down one day and compose in trancelike fashion the events of Jesus' life as dictated by God from heaven. Matthew relied on God, it is true, but he also relied very heavily on his fellow believers to help him write his Gospel. The finished product was really a three-way partnership venture involving Matthew, the body of believers and the Holy Spirit. If we fail to acknowledge the role of all three partners, we come up with a caricature rather than a true portrait of the Gospel.

Let us keep this "partnership" quality of the Gospels in mind as we begin now to analyze the Gospels of Matthew (Mt), Mark (Mk) and Luke (Lk), the first set of works we will explore in the second stage of New Testament development.

HOW THE SYNOPTIC GOSPELS DEVELOPED

Matthew, Mark and Luke are called the *Synoptic* Gospels. *Synopsis* literally means a comprehensive view or a perspective from which one is able to see an entire pattern emerging out of the composition of several parts.

What is it that makes the Synoptic Gospels synoptic? Generally speaking, we find in Matthew, Mark and Luke the same events in Jesus' life arranged in virtually the same order, as well as the treatment of common themes. The Gospel of John, on the other hand, takes a quite different approach. (Chapter Nine will explore *why* John is unique.)

The common pattern or development in all three Synoptic Gospels is as follows:
1) Prelude to Jesus' ministry (Mt 3:1—4:11; Mk 1:1-13; Lk 3:1—4:13)
2) Jesus' ministry in Galilee (Mt 4:12—18:35; Mk 1:14—9:50; Lk 4:14—9:50)

3) Jesus' ministry on the way to and within Jerusalem (Mt 19:1—20:34; Mk 10:1-52; Lk 9:51—18:43)
4) The passion and resurrection of Jesus (Mt 21—28; Mk 11—16; Lk 19—24)

Aside from this similarity in general pattern, there are other ways in which the Synoptics take a common approach to the life and ministry of Jesus:

First, there are many similarities in the language used by the Synoptic authors. Sometimes all three use virtually identical words in reporting an incident or a saying of Jesus. See, for example, the story of Peter's profession of faith (Mk 8:27-30; Lk 9:18-21; Mt 16:13-16).

Second, certain themes are grouped together in the same way in each Gospel. For example, each Gospel groups together stories about Jesus' attitude towards the Sabbath and, with some exceptions, each similarly positions collections of Jesus' parables.

Based on such evidence, Scripture scholars conclude that while the Synoptics undoubtedly derived much of their content from *oral* tradition—such as our imagined vignette beginning this chapter—they must have had common *written* traditions to rely on as well. What were these written traditions? Several theories attempt to answer this question.

Almost all scholars feel that the writers of Matthew, Mark and Luke used independent bits and pieces from the written sermons, teachings and stories of the first Christian preachers. These written bits of information about Jesus formed part of the primitive Christian kerygma or proclamation.

We have already read some of these bits and pieces of kerygma as they were incorporated by Luke—perhaps in unaltered form—into the main narrative of Acts. Peter's statement in Acts 2:38-39 is possibly Luke's verbatim use of an early Christian evangelist's standard homily.

Scholars also conclude that, in addition to the loose collection of writings derived from the primitive kerygma, the Synoptic authors used lengthier, more structured writings. Some scholars theorize, for example, that there was an early Gospel originally written in Hebrew (called "Proto-Matthew"), but now lost. The author of our Gospel of Matthew may have based his Greek manuscript on this document. (All English versions of the Gospels, and of the other New Testament books, have been translated from ancient Greek originals.)

Without entering into a lengthy discussion of the scholars' complex assertions and counter-assertions concerning the various written traditions underlying the Synoptics, we can simply summarize the most commonly held conclusion about the formation of the Synoptic Gospels.

This conclusion is based on the premise that Mark was written first, accounting for the large body of Marcan material appearing in Matthew and Luke.* Those portions of Matthew and Luke which do not rely on Mark, but which have the same verses in common with each other, are said to be based on a prior written source which is now lost and which is called simply "Q" (an abbreviation for the German word *Quelle*, meaning "source"). Those verses in any of the three Synoptics which have *no* parallels in the other two derive from portions of the primitive kerygma of which a particular author made sole use.

This approach to the evolution of the *written* Gospels combined with what we said earlier about *oral* traditions can be diagrammed roughly as follows:

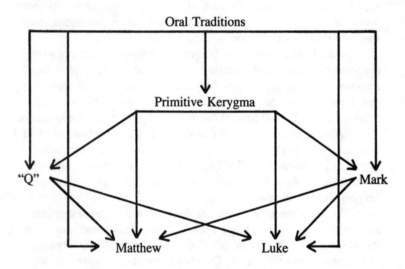

THE PERSONALITY OF EACH GOSPEL

The first disciples would not have understood the phrase "Synoptic Gospels," even though they were familiar with various written traditions about Jesus. They knew only *one* gospel—that of Jesus Christ. They heard the gospel proclaimed by different preachers with different backgrounds under different circumstances. Yet they were not so much concerned with various points of distinction in the message as they were in using what was proclaimed to change their lives.

---

*Of 673 verses in Mark, 600 appear substantially the same in Matthew, and about 350 appear substantially the same in Luke.

For the early disciples, then, the gospel was first and foremost "the power of God leading everyone who believes in it to salvation..." (Romans 1:16). Our purpose in analyzing the Synoptics is to discover the common source of power experienced by the first believers. Ironically, however, the more we explore the common features of the Synoptics, the more we discover that each book has its own unique "personality."

Let us look now at the Synoptics with a view toward determining the distinctive features of each Gospel. This exploration will help us see how each author moved the early disciples from infatuation to deeper intimacy with Jesus—the theme of the second stage of New Testament development.

Mark

Can we make an educated guess as to Mark's audience by sampling a few verses? In Mark 7:3-4 we read an explanation of the Pharisees' custom of washing their hands before eating. In 14:12 we read that "on the first day of Unleavened Bread..." it was "customary to sacrifice the paschal lamb." In 15:42 we find that the Jewish "Preparation Day" takes place on "the eve of the sabbath." What can we conclude from verses such as these? The answer is obvious—Mark was writing for an audience of non-Jews who were unfamiliar with Jewish customs.

Although Mark does not appear in the Gospels, he does appear in other New Testament books. Peter stays in the house of the mother of "Mark" (Acts 12:12). Paul and Barnabas take (presumably the same) Mark with them to Jerusalem (Acts 12:25), and later disagree about letting Mark (also known as *John* Mark) accompany them on a proposed missionary journey (Acts 15:37-39). Mark somehow became associated with Peter in early Church tradition. This tradition is reinforced by the reference to Mark in 1 Pt 5:13 as "my son." Presumably Mark served as Peter's close disciple, perhaps as his secretary. Mark wrote his Gospel sometime between 64 A.D. and 70 A.D.

His purpose in writing was to explain to his principally Gentile audience the identity and mission of the Jewish Messiah, Jesus of Nazareth. Because Mark was a Jew, he presented his teaching from a Jewish perspective. Yet he gave enough information to his Gentile readers so that they—aided by additional teachings from members of the Christian community—could understand the points he was trying to make.

Mark reveals Jesus' identity in stages. He does this in order to lead his readers to a painful conclusion—that the Messiah had "to suffer much, be rejected by the elders, the chief priests, and the scribes, *and* be put to death..." (Mk 8:31). Just as this was a difficult lesson for Jesus' disciples to accept (8:32), so too it would have been difficult for Mark's readers. The "folly of the Cross" was not something easy to accept then—or now.

To lead his readers to a level of understanding where they could accept the Cross in their own lives (Mk 8:34), Mark first establishes by abundant evidence in the first half of his Gospel (1:1—8:26) that Jesus is the "holy One of God" (1:24), given authority by the Father to perform the very works of God on earth (2:10). Yet Mark stresses how Jesus "kept ordering them sternly not to reveal who he was" (3:12). (For these "messianic secret" passages, see 1:44, 3:12, 5:43, 7:36, 8:26, 8:30 and 9:9).

Mark has Jesus do this so that the readers of the Gospel would not be so attracted to Jesus' miracles as to miss the deeper meaning of his identity as God's suffering servant. Mark is prompting his readers to ask, "What kind of Messiah is this anyway who performs miracles and then asks that they be kept secret? Does Jesus do this because he is calling me to a deeper relationship with him than would be possible if I were merely impressed by his miracles?"

In the second half of Mark's Gospel (8:27—16:20) we find that Jesus is indeed asking his audience to make a deeper commitment to him. Jesus asks nothing less than for them to have the same total abandonment to the Father's will that he himself has. While this will be difficult, "Everything is possible to a man who trusts" (9:23).

Thus, in the second half of Mark's Gospel, the fuller purpose of Jesus' miracles comes into focus. For the reader who is trying to "deny his very self, take up his cross and follow in [Jesus'] steps" (8:34), Jesus' miracles are a means of bolstering that person's faith, as he or she cries out, "I do believe! Help my lack of trust!" (9:24).

Mark's Gospel reveals the hardship and sacrifice demanded of the Christian who wants to grow from infatuation with Jesus to intimacy with him. Mark introduces a principle we will find again and again in second-stage writings: Intimacy with Jesus comes only after the surrender of one's own will to God's will.

Matthew
We have little difficulty in deducing the intended readers of Matthew when we discover that the Old Testament is quoted 41 times in this Gospel, as opposed to about half that many times in Mark. Obviously, Matthew was intended for readers who thoroughly understood the teachings of the Old Testament—Jewish Christians.

28

By the time this Gospel was written (perhaps as late as 80-85 A.D.) the apostle Matthew would have been well up in years, if he was still alive. Thus it seems the Gospel of Matthew was not written by the apostle Matthew. By attaching his name to this Gospel, the early Church meant to suggest that the material represents Matthew's teaching, or the teaching of a school of disciples who had been associated with the apostle. (This does not mean that Matthew is inauthentic—the Holy Spirit worked through *whoever* wrote the Gospel.)* More than likely the author wrote from Antioch or some other city with a large Christian community, someplace outside of Jerusalem but in proximity to Palestinian Jewish Christianity.

Like Mark, Matthew wants to reveal to his readers the identity of Jesus as Messiah and Son of God. More than Mark, Matthew stresses the Jewish disbelief in Jesus. Matthew wants his readers to realize that the longed-for Messiah came to his people, but his people failed—or refused—to recognize him. Thus for Matthew the messianic secret is reduced to a minor theme.

Matthew, however, places greater emphasis than Mark on Jesus' teaching ministry, with Jesus delivering five major teaching discourses. In contrast, Mark's development of Jesus' ministry is action-oriented: Jesus reveals himself through his deeds as much as through his words.

Matthew's emphasis on teaching is consistent with his interest in presenting Jesus as the new Moses—the new lawgiver who presents God's authoritative words to humanity. Just as Moses discourses at length throughout the Old Testament books of Exodus, Numbers and Deuteronomy, so too Jesus—who had come to fulfill the Law Moses promulgated (see Mt 5:17)—discourses before the people, delivering to them the new teaching of God's Reign.

Since Matthew wrote in a more settled, less threatened community than Mark, he was able to speculate about the normal, day-to-day interrelationships of Christians living in community. One of Jesus' discourses in Matthew (18:1-35) treats divisions within the Christian community, and Matthew is the only Gospel which uses the Greek word for "church"—*ekklesia* (16:18, 18:17).

A further reason for Matthew's interest in the Church was that he wanted to demonstrate that the Church was the "new Israel," the new people called by God to inherit God's promises to the Jews of old. Jesus as the new Moses and the body of Christian believers as the new Israel—these are the twin themes of Matthew's narrative.

---

*For convenience we will refer to the anonymous author of this Gospel as "Matthew" throughout the rest of this book.

Luke

As we saw in the last chapter, Luke wrote the combined work Luke-Acts. We have considered Acts first because it preserves intact much of the primitive kerygma predating the Gospels. In writing his Gospel, Luke appropriated much of that primitive kerygma and adapted it to the expanded theological purpose of his Gospel.

Like Mark, Luke was writing principally for Gentiles. Luke, however, finished Luke-Acts probably around the year 85 A.D. and, most scholars think, wrote in Greece. The more rationalistic climate of Greece, as well as the Greek traditions of democracy, personal freedom and civic discipline would help to explain many of Luke's themes—such as universal salvation, concern for the poor, the higher status of women and the need for self-denial.

In his Gospel Luke presents Jesus as on a great journey. Luke traces this journey back to its primordial beginning—to Jesus' conception in Mary's womb through the action of the Holy Spirit (1:35). Jesus begins his Spirit-impelled journey in earnest after receiving the public anointing of the Spirit on the day of his baptism by John (3:21-22). He then goes forth into Galilee and the surrounding regions and, finally, to Jerusalem. Jesus' journey culminates in his death on the cross, his resurrection and ascension.

But the journey does not end there. Luke saw the Church as continuing and fulfilling Jesus' journey. Like Jesus, the Church too begins its life and ministry through the action of the Holy Spirit (Acts 2); and like Jesus it suffers persecution and rejection at the hands of the Jews (Acts 4 ff). And just as Jesus in Luke is receptive to all peoples, so too the first evangelists in Acts spread the gospel to Gentiles as well as to Jews.

Luke-Acts is united by the common theme of God's power at work on earth through the Holy Spirit. Jesus' life and ministry are visible manifestations of the Spirit's activity, but Jesus is not to be the sole minister of the Spirit to others. Because Jesus' Kingdom is not fully established by the time of his ascension, it remains to his disciples to carry on his mission.

Luke uniquely weaves this theme of Jesus' Spirit-impelled journey toward the Father around a number of lesser themes:

1) Luke, more than Mark and Matthew, portrays Jesus as the savior of *all* peoples. Whereas Matthew traces Jesus' genealogy back to Abraham (Mt 1:1-17), Luke traces it to Adam (Lk 3:23-38)—thereby assuring Gentile readers that Jesus, the savior of all, shares *their* ancestry as well as that of the Jews.

2) More than Mark and Matthew, Luke depicts Jesus as having

a concern for the poor and for all those who had no status in the eyes of society. For this reason women have a more respected position in Luke than in Mark and Matthew.

3) Luke is greatly concerned with presenting God as a God of mercy. For that reason, perhaps, Luke is the only Synoptic author to include the stories of the prodigal son (15:11-32) and of Zacchaeus (19:1-10), as well as the incident of the sinful woman (7:36-50) and the parables of the lost sheep and the silver piece (15:1-10).

4) Luke is the most contemplative of the Synoptic authors. In several places in his Gospel, he places Jesus in prayerful solitude before the Father. And consistent with the asceticism that is the mark of a true contemplative, Luke has Jesus demanding of his followers complete renunciation of material goods. Luke's readers are told that they must leave everything (5:11) if they are to follow Jesus. They must deny their very selves (9:23). They must rely totally on God, not on possessions (12:22-31).

GROWING TOWARD INTIMACY WITH JESUS

Now that we have a brief overview of the Synoptics, let us take a quick look at two scriptural examples that show how these authors use their material to call their readers from infatuation to intimacy with Jesus. For such was the very purpose of the Synoptics and—as we shall see—of the other writings of the second stage of New Testament development.

Discourse on the Beatitudes

Both Luke and Matthew relied on an original document from the primitive kerygma, probably written in Aramaic. This document preserved and summarized Jesus' teachings on the theme of God's promised blessing for those who place their trust solely in him. Since we no longer have the original Aramaic document, we must rely on Matthew and Luke to give us *their* versions of this segment of the primitive kerygma.

Matthew's Version (5:1-12). Matthew situates Jesus' discourse "on the mountainside" (5:1). He does this in order to parallel his scene with the locus of Moses' reception of the Law on Mt. Sinai. Notice the solemnity of the occasion; it is as if Jesus has been waiting for just such a moment to deliver this important address. Notice too that Matthew's Jesus withdraws from the crowd, collecting his disciples around him as he begins his teaching. This is another means the author uses to emphasize the solemnity of the occasion.

31

Matthew has *nine* beatitudes. The formula "Blest are...," like much of Matthew's phraseology, relies heavily on the Old Testament. For example, "the sorrowing" (5:4) is reminiscent of "all who mourn" in Is 61:2; and "the lowly" (5:5) likewise suggests this same messianic prophecy. By alluding to the Old Testament, Matthew wants to emphasize to his Jewish readers that Jesus fulfills the ancient prophecies, that he is the hoped-for Messiah who will deliver God's Chosen People from their bondage.

But as Matthew makes clear in the remainder of the passage, the deliverance Jesus will bring is not necessarily equivalent to Jewish expectations. Jesus promises no sudden victory over the Jews' earthly oppressors. Rather, he promises a quiet, subtle, spiritual victory—pointing toward a future day and, ultimately, toward the final Day of the Lord when God will reverse the world's priorities and replace them with his own.

In God's Kingdom it is not the powerful and the oppressors who will triumph, but the "poor in spirit," the "sorrowing" and the "lowly." In God's Kingdom the victorious will not be those who have mastered the arts of intimidation, acquisition and domination, but those who "hunger and thirst for holiness," those who "show mercy," "the single-hearted" and the "peacemakers."

Matthew wants his readers to realize that, in Jesus, the scales of justice are being tipped in the opposite direction. The age of oppression is at an end, while the victory of the oppressed is near. Matthew's Jewish readers would have immediately recognized the prophetic and symbolic overtones of Jesus' words. They would have been forced to decide whether to accept Jesus and *his* conception of God's Reign, or to continue in *their* false expectations of a Messiah who would fulfill their desires for power and vengeance.

Matthew was in a sense asking his fellow Jewish Christians, "Are you willing to identify yourselves with Yahweh's poor, or do your sympathies really lie in the direction of wealth, power and fame?" Or, to put it another way, he was asking, "Do you really want to become intimate with Jesus? If so, here is the price you must pay."

Luke's Version (6:17-26). Luke's version of this discourse differs from Matthew's in several important respects. First of all, notice that the setting in Luke is not a mountainside but a "level stretch" (6:17) or plain. Luke's Jesus doesn't leave the crowds to go *up* the mountain; he comes *down* the mountain to be with not just his disciples, as in Matthew, but with "a large crowd of people," many of whom are foreigners.

Second, Jesus' discourse in Luke doesn't appear to be premeditated, and it is hardly a solemn or portentous event. Jesus' discourse seems to grow spontaneously out of his association with the crowds. In the same way that his healing power spontaneously "went out from him" (6:19), his discourse just naturally emanates from his lips.

These differences are consistent with Luke's purpose and style. He constantly presents Jesus as an approachable, merciful figure, someone who freely mingles with the people and understands them. Luke's portrait of Jesus was influenced by his own gifts of observation and intuition. Luke understood people's feelings, their inner psychological workings and secret motivations (see 3:15; 9:43; 18:9).

Perhaps because of this, Luke was less concerned with the spiritual overtones of Jesus' discourse than he was with the practical situations facing the persons whom Jesus addressed. Luke's Jesus is not the mountaintop master of Matthew's version, who issues his address from on high. Luke's Jesus is down in the midst of the suffering crowd. Notice that Matthew's Jesus refers somewhat aloofly to "the poor" while Luke's talks personally to "you poor."

Luke's Jesus sees his audience not as "poor in spirit" (Mt 5:3), but as "poor" (Lk 6:20). He is not concerned that the people "hunger and thirst for holiness" (Mt 5:6), but that they "hunger" (Lk 6:20b). In short, Luke's Jesus sees the people as they are; Matthew's Jesus sees them as they will one day become.

Both perspectives are important. If we were to emphasize only one Gospel to the exclusion of the other, we would miss the true teaching of the Beatitudes: that God is present *now* with his suffering poor, even though he has delayed the finality of their victory until some future time. So, while God's poor can confidently expect their *heavenly* reward, Jesus' disciples must at the same time not ignore their responsibilities to alleviate the poor's *earthly* suffering.

Luke makes it even clearer than Matthew which life-style Jesus' disciples are to choose by adding the four "woes" to his four Beatitudes. Readers of Matthew's version could erroneously conclude that in God's plan the wealthy could still rely on their riches and power while the poor are "catching up" to them. Luke makes certain his readers understand that it is *only* the poor, hungry, weeping and ostracized who are a part of God's Reign. He says *woe* to the "rich," the "full," those "who laugh," and to all the prestigious, famous people upon whom the world confers its power.

The human impossibility of fulfilling Jesus' demands becomes more obvious as both Matthew and Luke finish Jesus' discourse. At the end of each, the reader might feel like the disciples who ask elsewhere, "Then who can be saved?" (Mt 19:25). The answer is found in Jesus' response to those disciples' query: "For man it is impossible; but for

God all things are possible" (Mt 19:26). Only through God's mercy is anyone saved; humanity cannot save itself.

Matthew and Luke teach us the ultimate danger of riches: that in our wealth we become assured of our own power, merit and status. We feel that God owes us salvation because of our material achievements. Conversely, the blessing of poverty is that it renders us incapable of deluding ourselves as to our own merit in God's eyes. When we are poor we know that our efforts avail us nothing, that only God's power can save us. For this reason, both Matthew and Luke affirm, the Christian is called to a life of abandonment to God's providence.

Quite a challenge! After reading the two discourses on the Beatitudes, will we be capable of moving from infatuation with Jesus to intimacy with him?

Peter's Profession of Faith

Each author attaches great significance to this event, but it occupies more of a central place in Mark's plan (8:27-30) than in either Luke's (9:18-21) or Matthew's (16:13-20). Up to this point in Mark's Gospel, no one has openly professed a belief that Jesus is the Messiah. Jesus has given abundant evidence of his power over the natural elements and the spiritual powers of evil. Now, Jesus feels, it is time to see what—if anything—his trusted disciples have concluded about the early stages of his ministry.

"Who do people say that I am?" Mark's Jesus asks (8:27). (Note the divergence from Mt 16:13, "Who do people say that the Son of Man is?") The disciples tell Jesus that his ministry is reminiscent in the public mind of John's or even of Elijah's, whose return to earth was popularly expected (Malachi 3:23). Then Jesus turns the question pointedly toward his disciples and, by implication, toward Mark's readers. "Who do *you* say that I am?" In other words, Jesus is asking, "You say you love me and want to know me more intimately. Who, then, am I to you?"

Peter answers Jesus' question on behalf of the disciples, "You are the Messiah!" (Mk 8:29). As we saw in Chapter One, there were a variety of Jewish views about the Messiah. But Peter's response cuts through all the theories and comes right from the heart. His response is a spontaneous reaction to what must have been his own prior inner speculation about the identity of Jesus.

Peter's spiritual acumen lies not in giving the "right answer," but in having a heart disposed to receive the insight of God's revelation. Apparently this truth had been germinating in Peter's consciousness during the tenure of his relationship with Jesus. To put it another way, Peter was able to make the leap from infatuation to intimacy—the same leap we are all called to make.

We can never truly be intimate with our beloved unless we know our beloved's true nature and identity; and Peter's response to Jesus' question shows that we can truly know Jesus only after we yield to God's revelation. This is clearer when we read the response of Matthew's Jesus to Peter's answer (absent in both Mark and Luke): "Blest are you, Simon son of Jonah! No mere man has revealed this to you, but my heavenly Father" (Mt 16:17).

In Mark and Matthew Peter's profession is followed by Jesus' first prediction of his passion and death. Each author wants to emphasize that, while Jesus is the Messiah, he is at the same time the Suffering Servant of Yahweh. Thus, the significance of this passage for each author lies in the improbable notion of a suffering Messiah at the core of Christianity.

Matthew and Mark thus suggest that intimacy with Jesus will imply great sacrifice. Once again in this second stage of New Testament development we are told that the transition from infatuation to intimacy will not be easy. Yet our Synoptic authors challenge us to make that transition, telling us all the while that we will be called to follow our beloved down paths we might never have chosen had we not asked ourselves, "Who is Jesus of Nazareth?"

CHAPTER THREE

APOSTLE TO
THE GENTILES

**1 and 2 Thessalonians,
1 and 2 Corinthians**

Sunrise in the Nabataean desert is a time of transformation.
A brilliant fireball rising along the eastern horizon slowly scorches out
any trace of the cool, starlit universe which existed only minutes before.
Life during those first few moments of daylight is a time of adaptation.
Small rodents and other ground creatures scurry for cover. The sparse
plants adjust their posture and appearance as they begin their daily
exercise of cheating the arid wind of its few precious drops of
moisture.

Human life—what little there is of it in this wasteland—also
stirs to meet the morning's challenge of survival. A small settlement,
located near one of the lesser-visited oases east of Petra is already awake
and active. Seven or eight huts cluster around a central building where
the community's inhabitants gather. They are all men—perhaps 20 of
them—and they begin this day as they do all days, by praising their
God for his love and protection, and his fidelity to his promises.

After prayer the community disperses, each man going to his
assigned work. Some are engaged in construction projects to make room
for the ever-growing number of initiates into the community. Others
are engaged in making copies of the scrolls which the community guards
as its most precious possession.

The master of the community is an older man. His long beard
and thin hands suggest the demeanor of one devoted to study and the
pursuit of wisdom. Twenty years ago he and his closest friends had left
Jerusalem to found this community. They had been respected Doctors

37

of the Law—at the very pinnacle of their profession—when they suddenly announced their intention to forsake everything and come to this desert spot. Their colleagues had thought them mad, yet neither their friends, their families, nor these 20 years of isolation had deterred them from their purpose: to know and live the Word of Yahweh completely and perfectly.

Several months ago a man came to the community from Damascus seeking, as he put it, "a place to find God's direction for my new existence." The man had studied with the master years before in Jerusalem; at that time he found the master's emphasis on freedom as the Law's chief end challenging and alarming.

Yet here the man was, 20 years later, seeking the guidance of the same master. Something had happened to the man—something he could not fully comprehend. A sudden intuition assured him that the master was the only person who could answer his questions about the incident on the road to Damascus. "Master," he had pleaded during their first conversation some months ago, "tell me what this experience means!"

The master had listened intently as the man told him of the flash of light, the voice and his sudden blindness. When the man had finished the full story, the master sat quietly for some time and then spoke: "I do not know what this means, my son, but I do know that God has sent you here to learn the meaning. Stay with us and seek God's guidance. Together we will seek the meaning of this event for your life and for ours."

The man had lived with the community now for several months. Lately the master sensed that his guest's inner search was drawing to a close. So when the man arrives this morning for their talk, the master is not surprised to see him dressed for travel.

Motioning for the man to take a seat, the master asks, "Are you leaving us, my son?"

"Yes, Master, I have made some decisions. One of them is that I must return to Damascus. I feel that God would have me talk to others about my new understanding of his purpose for our people."

"I am not surprised. I am afraid I do not understand everything God has done for you, my son, or what he has in store for you now. Yet I know that he is calling you to proclaim something new to our people. You must follow what your heart is telling you."

"I will do that, Master, and I will carry with me the wisdom of your teaching. All these years I have struggled so hard. The Law has been a brutal tyrant for me. I understand now what you tried to teach me years ago: that God calls us not to slavery to the Law but to a life of freedom as his children. By God's will, I could not see it until I was struck blind."

"Unfortunately, my son," the master responds, "even in this desert spot, we are not truly free. We need a force external to ourselves to enable us to become free. I can see that you have found that force. You must take word of what you have found to others, and then return to us. Share with us what your travels teach you, my son. Let us know if our people accept that freedom of the children of God you proclaim to them."

PAUL—BEFORE AND AFTER

The word *apostle* comes from the Greek word *apostello*, meaning "to send." As Paul left the desert community that morning to begin his mission as one who was sent—by God, as well as by our imagined master—he undoubtedly had no idea of the amazing things God had in store for him.

Paul had been born in the city of Tarsus in the Roman Province of Cilicia. The Romans had made Tarsus a "free city"; thus Paul had certain privileges which other Jews living in the Empire did not have. The most important of these was Roman citizenship. Since Greek was the native tongue in Tarsus, Paul spoke Greek and probably preferred to read the Septuagint (Greek) version of the Hebrew Scriptures. He wrote all his letters in Greek as well.

Of course, like any good Jewish boy born outside of Palestine, Paul also had learned Hebrew. He must have developed a strong interest in Jewish traditions because, as a young man, he went to Jerusalem to study under the famous Gamaliel, one of the leading Jewish Masters of the Law.

Paul eventually became a rabbi of the Pharisee party. This made Paul a rabbi in a different sense than was Jesus. Jesus belonged to a class of "unofficial" rabbis who were called *rabbi* simply out of respect for their wisdom and because of their function as volunteer teachers in the synagogues. Paul, on the other hand, was admitted by ordination to the officially sanctioned class of rabbis. To achieve this, Paul had to satisfy rigorous educational requirements, be at least 40 years of age and married.

In addition to having at one time had a wife, Paul also had a sister (see Acts 23:16). Other than these details, we know little about Paul's early life.

Paul's real life—his life in Jesus Christ—began on the road to Damascus. He was headed there to arrest Christians or, as he would probably have called them at the time, heretics and lawbreakers. What happened on the Damascus Road (Acts 9:3-19; 22:6-16; 26:12-18) is not clear in every detail. What *is* clear, however, is that Paul met the risen Lord Jesus and was utterly transformed by the experience.

As suggested in our introductory vignette, a period of reflection is needed for one to internalize a sudden conversion experience. After Paul had been healed of his blindness by Ananias and had spent "some time" (Acts 9:19) in Damascus, he "went off to Arabia" (Galatians 1:17), the scene of our imagined story. "Later," he says, "I returned to Damascus. Three years after that I went up to Jerusalem to get to know Cephas [Peter]" (Galatians 1:17-18). Paul's trip to Jerusalem to get to know Peter and the other apostles led to his acceptance by the Church as a brother Christian and, eventually, as a full-fledged exponent of the gospel in his own right.

Paul's experience on the road to Damascus took place around the year 36 A.D. It is not until 15 years later that Paul's letter writing (at least as we have record of it) began.

PAUL'S WRITING

During his second missionary journey (c.51 A.D.), while in Corinth (Acts 18:1,18), Paul wrote his first letter to his recent converts in Thessalonica (Acts 17:1-9). During his third missionary journey Paul wrote more letters, probably while staying in Ephesus, to his recent converts in Galatia (c.54 A.D.), Philippi (c.56 A.D.) and Corinth (c.57 A.D.).

While traveling throughout Macedonia, Paul wrote again to the Corinthians (c.57 A.D.). And while in Corinth on a return visit to see what effect his letters had had on his flock, he wrote to the Church in Rome (c.58 A.D.). Imprisoned in Rome, Paul wrote at least three more letters—one to his friend Philemon and one each to the Churches at Collosae and Ephesus (c.61-63 A.D.). Paul died about the year 64 A.D. in Rome.

By this chronology we can see that all of Paul's writings were completed *before* the earliest of the Synoptic Gospels. Why, then, do we treat Paul's writings *after* the Synoptic Gospels?

Paul's writings have a purpose which is more expanded than that of the Synoptics. The Synoptics get down to basics. They present Jesus, the earthly Messiah, as he lived and worked among his disciples, proclaiming and bringing about the Kingdom of God. The Synoptics, then, establish the human image of the Messiah which was the prerequisite to all future evangelization.

Paul's writings for the most part *presume* this knowledge of Jesus' earthly ministry. As an evangelist he had no doubt preached some of the same stories about Jesus which were later recorded in the Synoptics. But Paul's main interest was to teach—in a different way than the Gospels were later to do—the significance of the *resurrected Jesus'* universal lordship. Paul did this in some letters by addressing specific problems facing various Churches which he pastored; in other letters he did this by writing abstract theological treatises.

Though Paul's letters predate the Synoptics, we consider them afterward because they appear to be later developments of Synoptic thought. Actually, both Paul's letters and the Synoptics are indebted to the primitive kerygma. Thus, in terms of chronology, both are—to use our original terminology—*second-stage* writings. As such they each have essentially the same purpose: to call the new Christian to make the transition from infatuation with Jesus to intimacy with him.

In this chapter we will discuss 1 and 2 Thessalonians (Thes) and 1 and 2 Corinthians (Cor).* These writings will give us a good look at both early Christian communal life and Paul's unique insight into the Christian vocation of intimacy with Jesus.

1 Thessalonians

Thessalonica was a city in the Roman Province of Macedonia. From Luke's account in Acts 17:1-9, we get the impression that Paul's mission there (and that of his comrade, Silas) lasted only "three sabbaths" (17:2). Probably Luke has shortened the actual time somewhat, since from 1 Thessalonians we get a picture of a community in which Paul has made deep friendships—of a type that would have taken several months to form.

Paul and Silas were forced by Jewish agitators to leave Thessalonica, so they moved to Beroea where they were joined by Timothy. Paul then traveled alone to Athens. While in Athens he had time to speculate about the condition of the fledgling Church he had just founded in Thessalonica, and he sent Timothy (who had rejoined him in Athens) to inquire. The First Letter to the Thessalonians is Paul's response to Timothy's report on the Thessalonian Church's condition.

This letter has a strong "eschatological" thrust to it; that is, it is much concerned with the "end times." (*Eschatology* comes from the Greek *eschaton*, or "last thing.") At this early phase of his apostolic

---

*The order of Paul's writings in the Bible have nothing to do with their respective dates of composition. They were apparently placed in an order based on their lengths, from longest to shortest.

career Paul believed, as did many early Christians, that the *Parousia* (or Second Coming) of the Lord was imminent.

Paul's principal teaching in 1 Thessalonians thus concerns the Parousia. Apparently some Thessalonians were worried about their friends and relatives who had already died. They evidently believed that when Jesus came in glory on the last day only those Christians who were then alive would be taken into heaven with him.

Paul dispels these fears by saying that Christians "who survive until [Jesus'] coming, will in no way have an advantage over those who have fallen asleep" (4:15). On the last day "those who have died in Christ will rise first. Then we, the living, the survivors, will be caught up with them in the clouds to meet the Lord in the air" (4:16b-17a).

The Thessalonians' concern about the Parousia had become rather extreme, so Paul has to bring them back down to earth. Like the Synoptic authors, Paul teaches that no one knows the "exact day or hour" (Mt 24:36) of the final day. As Paul puts it, "the day of the Lord is coming like a thief in the night." (1 Thes 5:20—Did Paul have access to Luke's source for this passage? See Lk 12:39.)

Also like the Synoptics, Paul stresses that the Thessalonians are to continue their normal Christian lives even while expecting the Lord's coming. They are not to isolate themselves from each other and neglect the demands of Christian love. Thus, especially in these last days, they are to "remain at peace with one another" (5:13b); "admonish the unruly; cheer the fainthearted; support the weak; be patient toward all" (5:14); "see that no one returns evil to any other; always seek one another's good" (5:15); "rejoice always, never cease praying" (5:17).

In 1 Thessalonians, then, Paul stresses that intimacy with Jesus does not lie in speculating about the end times and worrying about whether one has made it into the company of the elect. Rather, a maturing relationship with Jesus involves the often humdrum and mundane activities of serving the needs of others in one's daily work and prayer—even while awaiting the Lord's Final Coming.

2 Thessalonians

Many scholars see 2 Thessalonians as a work written not by Paul, but by someone who used the style, language and content of 1 Thessalonians to teach an equivalent message to a later audience. Notice that 2 Thessalonians exhibits certain "too obvious" similarities to its predecessor. For example, the opening verse reads like a quote of the opening verse of 1 Thessalonians.

Whoever wrote 2 Thessalonians, and for whomever it was intended, it is clear that Paul's teaching on the Parousia is continued there in an expanded fashion, yet in a fashion nonetheless consistent with the message of the first letter. Even though 2 Thessalonians seems clearly to date from a time after Paul's death, its similarity of purpose to 1 Thessalonians allows us to consider it along with other second-stage writings.

The author of 2 Thessalonians takes up the theme of the final day in such a way as to remind us of the Apocalypse of John (see Chapter Ten). The author tells his audience that the Day of the Lord cannot take place until "the mass apostasy" occurs and "the man of lawlessness" is revealed (2 Thes 2:3).

There could hardly have been "mass apostasy" in Paul's time when the young Church had just put down its roots. Likewise, the "man of lawlessness" or "antichrist" is a feature of later Christian thought not present in any other of Paul's writings.

Still, the author uses these two concepts to make the same point for his readers as Paul made in 1 Thessalonians: that his readers are not to let concern about the Parousia deter them from their daily Christian duties. "Therefore, brothers, stand firm" (2 Thes 2:15), the author says. "Hold fast to the traditions you received from us, either by our word or by letter."

Apparently the community addressed by the author of 2 Thessalonians spent so much time speculating about "the last day" that they didn't get any work done. In short, they were so spiritual that they weren't any earthly good. The author corrects such erroneous thinking by reminding his readers of Paul's own rule: "Anyone who would not work should not eat" (2 Thes 3:10).

1 and 2 Corinthians

Paul wrote 1 Corinthians from Ephesus about the year 57 A.D., some six years after he had left Corinth. He was motivated to write by a report he had received from a devout Corinthian convert named Chloe. By way of messengers to Paul in Ephesus, Chloe told Paul that serious disorders had arisen within the Corinthian community during Paul's absence. Paul was further prompted to write 1 Corinthians because of a letter delivered to him by certain members of the Church in Corinth about various doctrinal matters disputed within the community.

The First Letter to the Corinthians was not actually Paul's first letter to the Church in Corinth. He had written these Christians before, telling them among other things not to associate with immoral persons (see 1 Cor 5:9). In addition to this previous letter and to the letters we call 1 and 2 Corinthians, Paul wrote still another letter to this community.

Apparently Paul made a quick visit to Corinth as a follow-up to

43

his sending 1 Corinthians (see 2 Cor 12:14) and found that things were as bad as or worse than Chloe had reported. When he returned to Ephesus, Paul wrote the Corinthians a stern letter of reprimand (actually the *third* letter he had sent them), composing it "in great sorrow and anguish, with copious tears..." (2 Cor 2:4). After sending this letter, Paul sent Titus to Corinth to see if his reprimands had had any effect.

While Titus was in Corinth, Paul left Ephesus and traveled throughout Macedonia. Titus rejoined Paul, probably in Philippi, and reported to him that Paul's third letter did indeed have the desired effect. Paul was overjoyed to hear that many members of his Corinthian flock had accepted his written words of correction and that they desired to be reconciled with him. Paul then wrote 2 Corinthians—at least his fourth letter to them.

The Corinthian Church was plagued by factionalism. These factions were not necessarily organized around the Jewish-Gentile split within the community. (There were obviously more than just two factions in the Corinthian Church—see 1 Cor 1:10-12—so each faction must have included both Jewish and Gentile Christians.)

Nevertheless, the root of much of the Corinthian strife lay in the fact that certain Jewish Christians looked down upon the Gentile Christians. Some of these Jewish Christians caused serious problems for Paul because they claimed that he was not a "real" apostle like those in Jerusalem and that his ministry among the Corinthians had been invalid.

Paul's central purpose in his Corinthian letters was to unify and reconcile all the Corinthian Christians. He proceeds with the utmost delicacy, skill and tact—much like a parent trying to settle a quarrel among children. He seeks to correct the wrongs committed by each "child" but—like a wise parent—does not side with one child over another. So as not to risk intensifying the factional strife, he never names a given faction as he writes; he condemns sins without identifying specific sinners.

This approach in the Corinthian letters makes it difficult at times for us to know to whom Paul is speaking. He addresses persons who are poles apart in their thinking. For example in 1 Cor 6:18, he admonishes people who have not yet overcome their habits of sexual promiscuity. Yet just a few verses later, in 1 Cor 7:5, he is advising certain persons not to put undue emphasis on celibacy!

These two extremes of advice indicate both the complex nature of the divisions within the Corinthian community as well as the difficult task which confronted Paul the pastor. Instead of analyzing 1 and 2 Corinthians in detail, let us simply look at one important aspect of these letters which illustrates Paul's attempt to draw his flock into a more intimate relationship with Jesus.

PAUL'S FOCUS ON THE BODY

Paul takes up the theme of the body in two senses: (1) body in relationship to spirit and (2) the Church as body.

Body Versus Spirit

Paul alludes throughout much of 1 and 2 Corinthians to the problem which arose in the Corinthian community over the Greek perspective on the human body as opposed to the Hebrew perspective. The Jews looked upon the human person as an integrated whole; concepts of division such as "body," "soul" and "spirit" were foreign to them. Thus the Jews believed that God saved the whole person.

The concept of the body dying and the soul going on to further existence was extremely hard for them to comprehend. This explains why early Christian communities such as the Thessalonians (composed of many former Jews) worried about not being alive at the time of the Parousia. If their bodies (their total personhood) were dead, they reasoned, how could Jesus take them into heaven?

Opposed to the Jewish concept of the unity of the person was the Greek idea of duality. According to Greek philosophy the human person was divided into body and soul, or body and spirit, with the spiritual element considered of more worth than the body. The spirit was thought to be the seat of all the mental and emotional powers, while the body was thought to be merely the instrument which carried out the spirit's directives.

This type of thinking led to two extremes. Proponents of one extreme believed that since the spirit was superior to the body, anything having to do with the body was of no value—particularly the "baser" desires such as sex. These people frequently withdrew from ordinary society and concentrated only on "spiritual" matters.

Paradoxically, proponents of the other extreme started from the same premise, but came to an antithetical conclusion. They reasoned that since only spirit is of value, what we do with our bodies is of no lasting importance. Therefore, we may as well enjoy our bodies to the utmost, because the spirit lives on unaffected by any consequences of bodily action. This group tended toward hedonism, especially in the area of sexual conduct.

In 1 and 2 Corinthians Paul is writing to groups influenced by these contrasting understandings of the human body. To the

45

hedonists—those who proclaimed, "Everything is lawful for me" (1 Cor 6:12)—Paul writes,

> You must know that your body is a temple of the Holy Spirit, who is within—the Spirit you have received from God. You are not your own. You have been purchased, and at a price. So glorify God in your body. (1 Cor 6:19-20)

Paul wants to teach this group that the human body is not just so much physical matter, but that it is a special creation, filled with God's own Spirit. Indeed, so intimate is the relationship between Christ and the Christian that the human body is to be looked upon as part of the body of Christ, one of Christ's "members" (1 Cor 6:15). And "whoever is joined to the Lord becomes one spirit with him" (6:17).

Paul thus raises the Greek understanding of spirit to a level that encompasses the divine Spirit of the Lord. And since he teaches that the body is the temple of the Spirit, Paul likewise raises the status of the body to a more dignified level—where sexual promiscuity and other misconduct are seen as degrading.

To those Corinthians who denigrate sexuality, on the other hand, Paul likewise has corrective advice. This group had written him hoping he would encourage them in their plans to terminate their marriage commitments by becoming celibate—a state of life they regard as "pure," in opposition to the sexually active married state.

Paul's "general rule" to these people is that "each one should lead the life the Lord has assigned him, continuing as he was when the Lord called him" (1 Cor 7:17). Thus husband and wife should continue to have sexual relations (1 Cor 7:3) "unless perhaps by mutual consent" (7:5) they should refrain for a while to devote themselves more fully to prayer.

The Church as Body

The climax of Paul's teaching on the body in the second sense—that of the community of believers—is found in 1 Cor 12—14. Certain persons in Corinth had gotten "carried away" with the gifts of the Holy Spirit. The ecstasy of their infatuation with Jesus had led them to focus almost all of their energies on the joyous emotions which had suddenly erupted in their lives. They had become so fascinated with these spiritual consolations that they had started to neglect their duties to the body of believers. Further, one person would assert his or her spiritual experience as superior to another person's.

Paul wrote to correct these errors, urging his readers to grow from infatuation to a deeper relationship with Jesus. He does this by clarifying, first, the purpose of spiritual gifts and, second, the relative importance of each gift to the community.

To accomplish his purpose, Paul uses the analogy of the body (1 Cor 12:12-26). He urges the Corinthians to put their newfound gifts to use in the same harmonious fashion that the human body regulates and coordinates its various organs. No Christian is unimportant, Paul stresses; the body needs everyone. For, "If all the members were alike, where would the body be?" (1 Cor 12:19). Each person must put his or her particular gift to work for the common welfare, for the good of the body of Christ (12:27). Within this body are certain functions which are graded according to importance (12:28-30), but the body as a whole suffers if it lacks even the humblest function.

Paul grades the various gifts of the Holy Spirit in order of importance. For example, the gift of prophecy outweighs the gift of tongues, since prophecy builds up the Church while tongues builds up only oneself (1 Cor 14:4). By instructing the Corinthians on the purpose of the gifts they each possess and urging them to use these gifts for the upbuilding of the Church, Paul shows them how to grow from infatuation to intimacy with the Lord.

DIFFERENT APPROACHES, SAME CHALLENGE

Perhaps now it is easier to understand what we meant earlier when we said that both the Synoptics and Paul accomplish the same purpose through different methods. Paul and the Synoptic Mark, for example, each teach the virtue of self-sacrifice, but in a vastly different way. Paul calls the Corinthians to leave behind their obsessive desires (whether sexual or celibate) and to put others' needs before their own. He achieves this not by quoting Jesus or by depicting a scene from Jesus' ministry; Paul simply "preaches" to the Corinthians, using language which is at different times theoretical and practical, abstract and concrete.

Mark, on the other hand, gives an equivalent teaching on self-sacrifice by quoting a saying of Jesus:

> "If a man wishes to come after me, he must deny his very self, take up his cross, and follow in my steps. Whoever would preserve his life will lose it, but whoever loses his life for my sake and the gospel's will preserve it." (Mk 8:34-35)

Despite the different approaches, both of these second-stage writers issue the same challenge: Infatuation with Jesus is not enough. Although the cost of discipleship is great, it is only by paying that price that one reaches a more intimate relationship with Jesus.

CHAPTER FOUR

JUSTIFICATION BY FAITH IN JESUS CHRIST

Philippians, Galatians

Everyone said the merchant had amassed a great fortune since the day he had taken over his father's silk brokerage house. The merchant had a knack for business, it was true, but he had also been blessed with good fortune. The number of ships entering Corinth's harbor annually during the 10 years since his father's death had more than tripled.

The merchant spent months each year traveling throughout Asia, Bithynia, Pontus and Cappadocia. Every other year he traversed the Persian deserts to attend the great bazaars held near the source of the Amu Darya, where merchants of every race on earth met to exchange their wares.

The merchant's business success was built on his talent for adaptation—not only to the changing religious practices he encountered, but adaptation as well to the moral traditions of each land he visited. In his travels he was eager to follow the customs of his hosts, particularly in the area of relationship with women.

Just as the sharing of a cup of tea, a meal, or the exchange of gifts served to lessen the harshness of travel and place businessmen who did not know each other on more cordial terms so, too, did the casual sharing of women. If anyone had suggested to the merchant another mode of conduct, the merchant would have considered him a fool.

Given the merchant's long-standing adaptation to the sexual promiscuity of the Eastern lands, it came as a shock to his friends when,

49

upon his return from a lengthy trip, he refused to accompany them to their favorite brothel. An even greater shock was hearing him renounce his former way of life and pledge henceforth to have sexual relations with none other than an unknown woman "he prayed God would send him." They listened in stunned silence as he recounted a story more bizarre than any he had told before.

Struck with a painful stomach disorder, he had been forced to lay over for two weeks in Ancyra in central Galatia. One day he had decided to stretch his legs with a little walk and found himself on the outskirts of the town near the Jewish synagogue. The little building was too small to contain the large crowd which had gathered to hear an itinerant Jewish teacher.

The Jew was of medium stature, balding, dressed rather plainly. He spoke with little eloquence, yet the merchant had listened closely to every word, attracted more by the speaker himself than by his mysterious words. The Jew seemed to turn his gaze directly toward the merchant as he said, "Don't you know that your bodies are God's own temple, the very building where God dwells through his Spirit?"

As the merchant finished his tale, his friends sat silently until one man spoke. "I cannot imagine a god who requires a man to limit himself to a single woman. He must be a foolish and weak god. I leave you to your foolishness. Should you need me, you can find me at the brothel!"

Several other men laughed at their comrade's remark and followed him out the door. Two other men stayed behind. They asked the merchant to tell them more about what the Jew had said.

Two years passed since the merchant had returned from his life-changing trip. Through his many contacts in the cities of Macedonia and Asia he heard reports of the Jew's visits to other cities. The merchant kept alive his hope that someday the Jew and his companions would come to Corinth.

One day the merchant hurried excitedly to the house of a Jewish couple who had frequently shared with him their table and their thoughts. "He is coming!" he announced. "I heard that he was in Athens just two days ago. When he arrives, will you please offer him your home for a few days? He will not remember me, and I am not a Jew. He will feel more comfortable with you. I will send my servant on the road to fetch him."

When the Jew arrived the couple took him into their home. His visit of a "few days" lasted for nearly two years. During this time the Jew—the "master," as he came to be called—frequently met with the merchant to discuss various questions the latter had. One day the merchant showed up for his meeting very dejected.

"What is troubling you, my friend?" the Jew asked.

"Master," the merchant responded, "you have taught us about the freedom of the children of God. You have said that God has given us his own Spirit to fight against the powers of darkness. Why then does my body long for its old ways? While I don't return to the brothels, inwardly I desire to do so. Has God not sent his Spirit upon me as you said? Why then has God not set me free from this power at work within my body?"

The Jew looked intently at the merchant for a few seconds and then spoke.

"My friend, I can see there is more I must teach you. When you received the Holy Spirit two years ago in Galatia, God truly set you free from the power of sin. Yet God does not overwhelm us with his freedom. True freedom is purchased at a price. Just as God's Son suffered to earn our freedom for us, so too must we suffer through growing pains after our new birth to freedom.

"If God simply substituted his power for our own, that would not truly be freedom. God wants us to adapt ourselves to his power so that it truly becomes a part of our lives, and that takes time, my friend. Until that happens, you must suffer patiently each day as your natural body continues to die to the power of sin."

"But, Master," the merchant asked, "isn't there some *method* I could undertake to achieve true freedom from sin? Some of my Jewish friends have said that your Jewish Law teaches how to make oneself holy—through circumcision, fasting, cleansing oneself and keeping the holy days. Would not these things help me to become free?"

The Jew shook his head and answered softly, "These men are wrong, my friend. There is no method to freedom but the Spirit. We become free not by doing *more*, but by doing *less*; not through our own efforts, but by surrendering to God's action in our life. That is what distinguishes our new way from the Jewish Law. Do not accept the way of the Law, my friend; choose the way of the Spirit."

HOW DOES ONE BECOME FREE?

As our story suggests, the apostle Paul was led by circumstances arising during his missionary travels to speculate a good deal about Christian freedom. The theme of freedom dominates three of his letters—Philippians (Phil), Galatians (Gal) and Romans (Rom).

Having had a profound experience of Christian liberation, Paul was in a good position to speculate on the nature of Christian freedom.

During the first half of his adult life, he had submitted himself totally to a religious system based on rigid attention to personal sanctification. The Pharisaical system which Paul followed was in many ways a perversion of Judaism; yet many had come to think of it as the best Judaism had to offer.

We get a taste of the burdensome nature of Paul's way of life in Matthew's Gospel. Jesus compares the minute requirements of the Pharisaical religious system which Paul practiced to "heavy loads, hard to carry" (Mt 23:4b). Paul carried these heavy loads until Jesus appeared to him on the road to Damascus and took them from his shoulders. Beginning at that moment, Paul sensed deep within his heart the words,

> "Come to me, all you who are weary and find life burdensome, and I will refresh you. Take my yoke upon your shoulders and learn from me, for I am gentle and humble of heart. Your souls will find rest, for my yoke is easy and my burden light." (Mt 11:28-30)

As Paul grew to a deeper understanding of his own liberation in Christ, he was more and more motivated to share with others the effects of this liberation. One could summarize Paul's ministry as an effort to persuade others to accept Jesus' easy yoke, to discover freedom in Christ.

This is Paul's major contribution to the second stage of New Testament development. He wants his readers to understand that the transition from infatuation to intimacy results in a freedom which releases one from the bondage of self and the imprisonment of the Law (a term used by Paul in a very specific sense, as we shall soon see).

Paul's vehemence in refuting the "Judaizers" (Jewish Christians who sought to impose upon other Christians the dictates of the Law) is a common theme in Philippians, Galatians and Romans. Paul's message in these books is directed to those who sought to pervert Christianity in his day. But it speaks just as clearly to those who, centuries later, would reduce Christianity to a regimen of self-development where one aspires to salvation by scrupulously keeping "the rules."

As we shall see, Paul does not throw out the rules. Rather, he restores them to their proper place, as subsidiary to and supportive of what is most important in Christianity—one's inner transformation into a new creation in Christ. Paul makes it clear that rules avail nothing in bringing about this transformation. The extent to which modern Christianity concentrates on rules instead of spiritual transformation is the extent to which it distorts Paul's teaching.

Let us now take a brief look at Paul's instruction on Christian freedom as we discuss Philippians and Galatians. (We will reserve a discussion of Romans for the next chapter.)

Philippians

Paul had first visited Philippi during his second missionary journey, probably around the year 50. He had first been inspired to venture into Macedonia (the Roman province in which Philippi lay) by a vision he had in Troas in Asia. In this vision, "a man of Macedonia stood before him and invited him, 'Come over to Macedonia and help us'" (Acts 16:9b).

The Philippian Church was Paul's first major "conquest" on European soil. Perhaps because his mission to Philippi had been a ground-breaker for the entire western thrust of his evangelistic activities, he always looked back with fond memories on his Philippian days. These memories were even fonder because of the Philippians' open and generous spirit in accepting both Paul and his gospel. The Philippians probably remained Paul's favorite community among all of those he visited.

Paul wrote to the Philippians on several occasions while in the city of Ephesus. Paul had returned to Ephesus during his third missionary journey and lived there for three years (Acts 20:31), probably the years 54-57. We saw earlier that Paul wrote 1 Corinthians from Ephesus; he likely wrote Galatians from Ephesus also.

There are actually three letters stitched together in our Letter to the Philippians. A later editor snipped bits and pieces from each letter to join the best features into one composite.

The 'First' Letter. While opinions vary (a minority of scholars do not accept the three-letter hypothesis at all), what is generally considered to be the "first letter" in Philippians is found in Phil 4:10-20.

In this segment Paul expresses his joy at the Philippians' generosity in contributing to his upkeep, both earlier while he evangelized the Thessalonian community (4:16), and again now while he is in Ephesus experiencing certain undefined "hardships" (4:14). The Philippians' second contribution has been brought to Paul by Epaphroditus, who apparently took sick in Ephesus and had to stay with Paul awhile before he could return to Philippi (2:25-28).

The 'Second' Letter. This is generally considered to be found in Phil 1:1—3:1a; 4:4-7; and 4:21-23. In this letter Paul discusses his "imprisonment in Christ's cause" (1:13). We don't know why Paul was in jail—perhaps because of the disturbance caused by the Ephesian silversmiths (Acts 19:23-40) who feared that Paul's preaching would hurt their idol-making business. These silversmiths may have brought charges against Paul and taken him to court (Acts 19:38) where Paul came out the loser.

Paul's imprisonment gave him time to reflect on the sufferings associated with spreading the Gospel. He had become dejected at all the things that had gone wrong during his apostolate—so much so that he began to long for his death and eternal reward with Christ. Yet he realized the need for continuing his ministry, and thus resolved to persevere through his sufferings for the sake of his beloved Philippians (1:21-26).

The twin themes of the second segment of Paul's Philippian correspondence are the unity of the body of believers and the corresponding need for individual self-sacrifice for the sake of this body, themes which are likewise the essence of 1 and 2 Corinthians. Paul begs his beloved Philippians to "make my joy complete by your unanimity, possessing the one love, united in spirit and ideals. Never act out of rivalry or conceit; rather, let all parties think humbly of others as superior to themselves, each of you looking to others' interests rather than his own" (2:2-4). As a perfect model for the Philippians on self-sacrifice for the good of others, Paul holds up the example of Jesus himself (2:6-11).

The 'Third' Letter. Paul learned from Timothy that certain new preachers who had arisen in Philippi were preaching a false gospel and tearing the community apart. Paul realized that the moderate tone of his second letter had availed nothing. So in his third letter (3:1b—4:4, 8-9) he spares no invective to condemn the false teachers.

The Jews had a special epithet to express their prejudice against Gentiles—"dogs." Paul thus refers to the false teachers as "unbelieving dogs" (3:2) in order to make the Judaizers among the false teachers feel especially insulted. He refers to these Judaizers as "those who mutilate," that is, those who teach that the Jewish requirement of circumcision is binding on new Christians.

Paul makes it clear that "external evidence" (3:4) such as circumcision matters not at all in earning salvation or rightstanding before God. If it did, Paul could certainly boast of his many external signs—his circumcision, his Hebrew origins, his Pharisaical background and his scrupulous attention to the Law. But he humbly acknowledges that "the justice I possess is that which comes through faith in Christ" (3:9b).

As Paul will explain more intricately in Romans, the liberating effect of one's being made just by Christ is not an instantaneous experience. Rather, Christians must allow God's resurrection power to transform their lives gradually. Paul says,

> "Brothers, I do not think of myself as having reached the finish line....All of us who are spiritually mature must have this attitude....It

is important that we continue on our course, no matter what stage we have reached." (Phil 3:13a, 15a, 16)

These words would no doubt have been of solace to the merchant we imagined at the beginning of this chapter. Paul prudently taught that it is not easy to grow from infatuation with Jesus to intimacy with him, and that patience is required. Paul's writings were intended to assist those who found the growth process from stage to stage painful.

In order to understand how Paul sees this process of Christian growth from infatuation to intimacy and identity with Christ, we need to become more familiar with three concepts: *justice*, *faith* and *law*. We have already touched on these concepts as they are found in the third segment of the Philippian correspondence. We will discover that they appear repeatedly in Galatians and Romans. So before proceeding to these next two letters, let us define what Paul means by these concepts.

'JUSTICE,' 'FAITH' AND 'LAW'

The Greek word Paul uses in his writings for justice is *dikaiosyne*. In his context the word is perhaps better translated as "uprightness" or "rightstanding." For Paul as for all Jews, no one is upright but God. The question he addresses in Philippians, Galatians and Romans is: How does one share in God's uprightness, that is, how does one become "just"?

The Judaizers erroneously thought that one becomes just by keeping the dictates of the Law—a term used by Paul in several different connotations. But Paul's primary use of *Law* is as the teaching preserved in the first five books of the Old Testament and the human-made religious rules arising from these books.

Paul answers the question of how to become "just"—how one is transformed from non-uprightness to uprightness—more fully in Romans (see Chapter Five). So we will not discuss this "justification" process at length here. It is important, however, to note at the outset how Paul viewed the state of justice and uprightness which humanity achieved in Christ.

For Paul, humanity was not simply *declared* to be upright; humanity was actually *made* upright by God through Jesus' death and resurrection. There is a tremendous difference between these two propositions. If God merely *declared* humanity to be just, as if merely putting a new name on the same old reality, then we are not really empowered by God to become the new creations which Paul describes in his writings. Instead, humanity is the same old humanity, powerless to become anything better than it is. But Paul saw humanity as actually being *made* just, so that we in reality became empowered to live a vitally new type of existence.

These two viewpoints on justification have rivaled each other during the centuries since Paul's time. The former viewpoint has led to a Christianity which sees itself in a "holding pattern," with no other mission than to wait for God to accomplish the final act in salvation history. Until then, Christians are to concentrate on being good and observing various rules of conduct so as to entitle themselves for entrance into heaven.

The other viewpoint on justification—Paul's viewpoint—sees Christianity as a community of individuals empowered by God to change themselves and material creation into an ever-increasing manifestation of God's presence on earth. In this view, Christians are not to focus on earning their way to heaven by adhering to religious rules, but on spreading to others the resurrection power released by Jesus, and thus helping these others to become free.

The catalyst which transforms the Christian into a state of justice—and thus of freedom—is faith. The Greek word Paul uses for faith is *pistis*. He does not mean by this word simply "belief" or "assent"; he means something closer to "acceptance" as indicated by *demonstrable signs* in the life of one who professes belief. Thus, one does not become upright before God simply by saying, "I believe," even though for some that may be a starting point. To express faith in Jesus requires a surrender of one's *entire person* to the lordship of Jesus.

It would have been inconceivable to Paul for a person to say, "Jesus is Lord," without demonstrating in his or her life the love for Jesus and Jesus' disciples that such a faith proclamation presupposed. As we have seen, Paul acknowledges that different persons are at different stages of development in their faith, and thus he knows that faith itself is a continuing process. Yet, as the believer's faith grows, Paul expects his or her deeds of love to grow commensurately. For Paul, this would be a sure sign that a Christian was growing from infatuation with Jesus to intimacy.

Galatians

Galatia was the Roman province located in what is today the nation of Turkey and, more specifically, that portion of Turkey known as Anatolia. The Letter to the Galatians is the only one of Paul's letters not addressed to a particular community or individual.

Scholars are divided over the question of Paul's intended audience. One group sees the audience as northern Galatian (and thus largely non-Jewish) Christians living in and around the cities of Ancyra, Tavium and Pessinus. Another group of scholars sees the audience as Christians in south Galatia who lived principally in the cities of Derbe, Lystra and Iconium.

In these southern cities there was a larger Jewish community than in the three northern cities Paul visited. The content of Galatians seems to support the southern viewpoint: The letter presupposes a deeper knowledge of Judaism than would have existed among the northern Galatian cities where Jewish customs were scarcely known at all.

Paul encountered a difficulty in Galatia that he likewise had encountered in Corinth. Judaizers in Galatia disparaged Paul's credentials as an apostle. He thus begins Galatians by launching into a defense of his apostolic calling. As in 1 and 2 Corinthians, Paul's apologia is rich in personal details about his life and personality. He asserts that his gospel was not something he learned from mere mortals. Rather, "it came by revelation from Jesus Christ" (Gal 1:12b).

Paul relates a previous incident to illustrate that he is an authentic apostle in his own right. He tells of how he once accosted Peter on the question of the Judaizing tendencies present among some Christians. Peter had come to Antioch, where Paul had headquartered himself, and had been eating openly with Gentile converts until associates of James arrived from Jerusalem. Because of their example Peter quit eating with the Gentiles and segregated himself from them, along with James's associates.

Paul admonished Peter to his face, telling him he had no right to "force the Gentiles to adopt Jewish ways" (2:14b). His point in relating the incident is that only another apostle could have publicly confronted the chief apostle with erroneous behavior.

Paul also uses the story of his corrective advice to Peter as a springboard for his central teaching in Galatians—namely, "that a man is not justified by legal observance but by faith in Jesus Christ" (2:16a). Through certain Old Testament examples Paul exhorts his readers not to return to their former reliance on "works." He reminds the Galatians:

> It was for liberty that Christ freed us. So stand firm, and do not take on yourselves the yoke of slavery a second time!...Any of you who seek your justification in the law have severed yourselves from Christ and fallen from God's favor! (Gal 5:1,4)

Yet Paul cautions the Galatians against going to the other extreme and turning their freedom into libertinism. By Christian freedom Paul does not mean "a freedom that gives free rein to the flesh" (Gal 5:13a), but a freedom that makes one available to serve others (5:13b).

Thus, for Paul, freedom is not "freedom *from*" but "freedom *for*"—freedom for greater service to the body of believers so that the unity of that body is built up and preserved. These works of service are not to be equated with the "works" which Paul elsewhere condemns. The works of Christian service are not a *means* used to gain one's acceptance by God in Christ, but the results of that acceptance expressed through faith.

The error of the Judaizers lay in their teaching that works—especially observances of the Jewish Law—would *merit* one's justification by God. In refuting this error, Paul did not seek to do away with all religious works—especially works of loving service. He simply wanted to emphasize that these works do not merit justification but rather are a sign that one's justification has already taken place.

Another sign that justification has taken place in one's life is shown in the type of moral behavior which one exhibits. Paul equates the state of justification with life in the spirit, and the state of living according to the Law with life in the flesh. By "flesh" Paul means not the sexual appetite, but the tendency of human nature to gravitate toward the baser aspects of life. The "flesh" is thus a state of non-freedom, while the "spirit" is the state of freedom.

Paul lists examples of these baser aspects in Gal 5:19-21a, and he lists characteristics of the life of Christian freedom in Gal 5:22-23. He was not so naive as to expect Christians instantaneously to eliminate all the vices contained in the first list and replace them with the virtues in the second list. He knew that different people are in different stages of development. What was important to Paul was that everyone tried to make progress, and that the strong helped the weak to grow (Gal 6:1-2). He closes Galatians by succinctly restating his central theme: "It means nothing whether one is circumcised or not. All that matters is that one is created anew" (6:15).

Having discussed Paul's thoughts on Christian freedom in Philippians and Galatians, we now see that the transformation from infatuation to intimacy—the theme of writings of the second stage of New Testament development—has taken on a new dimension. Earlier we saw that death to self is a necessary aspect of that transformation. Now we see that there is a reward for our dying, something Paul will call in Romans "the glorious freedom of the children of God" (8:21). Let us explore the theme of Christian freedom more deeply as we turn now to that work which, more than any other, qualifies as Paul's masterpiece.

CHAPTER FIVE

'THE GLORIOUS FREEDOM OF THE CHILDREN OF GOD'

Romans

Paul was an older and wiser man when he began to compose Romans. His expectations about human nature had been refined in the cauldron of controversy—with Judaizers and others. He had suffered physical and psychological abuse and sensed that grave peril awaited him on his return to Jerusalem.

Feeling the full weight of the cross he bore in Jesus' name, yet filled with the joy of the Spirit's ever-increasing manifestation in his life, Paul decided to take time off from the missionary circuit to write a treatise reflecting his complete understanding of the Christ event. His Letter to the Romans is that treatise.

Paul wrote Romans from Corinth, where he had returned after completing his Corinthian correspondence. The probable date is 58 A.D.; its audience is a mixed community of Gentile and Jewish Christians. Although the letter is addressed "to all in Rome" (1:7), it is likely it was a circular letter read first in several Churches Paul had founded, and then sent on to the Roman Church, which Paul had not founded.

For some time Paul had longed to go to Rome (1:10-13), and it is possible that he addressed the letter to the Roman community as an act of commitment to finalize his plans. He hoped that his teaching would be well-known in Rome before he arrived, so that he could dispense with preliminaries when he began evangelizing in person.

Romans is the very heart of the second stage of New Testament development. More than any other work it discusses what we could call, for lack of a better word, the "mechanics" of salvation. It emphasizes a most important element in the growth from infatuation to intimacy: *understanding*.

A simple analogy will perhaps explain this. Two persons who have grown intimate by their love—a husband and wife, let's say—find that each has a need to know and understand what really matters most in the other's life. For example, if both lovers are engaged in professional careers, each feels a need for the other to understand and appreciate the demands and challenges of his or her daily life at the office, or in the classroom, hospital or other setting.

Nothing dampens a love relationship more than for one partner to yawn every time the other discusses something challenging and exciting in his or her career. While neither partner will become an expert in the other's professional pursuits, there is nonetheless a strong desire for *understanding* by the partner of one's interests and accomplishments.

In the same way, unless we *understand* what Jesus Christ accomplished by his life, death and resurrection and how he accomplished it, we are not likely to grow very intimate with him. In Romans Paul defines Jesus' accomplishment—telling us both the meaning of and the means by which we have attained our freedom in Christ. In Romans Paul seeks to add understanding to our faith, so that we can better appreciate the meaning of our beloved's life.

Romans will likely appear to us as very "theological" and (with the possible exception of Hebrews and Revelation) may be the most difficult of all New Testament works to read. If we accept Thomas Aquinas's definition of theology—"faith seeking understanding"—we will, perhaps, approach Romans with less trepidation. Since Romans is the key to understanding Paul's other second-stage writings, we will analyze this work in more detail than Paul's other letters.

PAUL'S GOSPEL

Paul introduces himself to the Romans by telling them something of his apostolic ministry. God has set him apart from others, he says, to proclaim "the gospel of God" (1:1). Notice that he does not say "the gospel of Jesus Christ." Paul wants to suggest to his readers that he will be describing the mysterious and long-hidden purposes of the Father as they are now being revealed to humanity.

This emphasis is consistent with Paul's teaching that the Father had planned before the dawn of time to bring humanity to salvation in Christ—a theme he will develop further in Romans. This gospel, Paul says, was foreshadowed in the Old Testament (1:2) and concerns God's Son, who was descended from David in his humanity but was made

"Son of God in power" (1:4) through his resurrection.

Right from the start, then, Paul establishes that his writing will concern not a defeated and crucified carpenter from Galilee, but a powerful *kyrios* ("lord"). Not only is this *kyrios* powerful in himself, but the gospel concerning him likewise empowers its hearers. Paul calls this gospel "the power of God leading everyone who believes in it to salvation..." (1:16).

In Rom 1:18—3:20 Paul wants to establish how humankind, unsubmitted to God and left to its own devices, imperils itself. His graphic description of this sad condition is a necessary contrast to his later discussion of how God has empowered humanity to overcome its natural tendency toward evil.

He thus begins by painting a stark picture. Perversity, idolatry, conceit, animalistic lust, greed, envy, murder and insolence are the natural human tendencies which Paul sees operating in a world where God's justice—his uprightness—does not predominate.

Paul is not simply describing a particular historical era in these passages. He is describing the life of every man and woman who has not been made just, or upright, by God. Or, to put it another way, he is describing a stage of existence preceding infatuation—the first stage in the love relationship of those who accept Jesus as Lord.

By "sin" Paul means more than immoral actions. He also means a force existing within humanity leading it to death and destruction. He will shortly contrast the effects of this negative power with the liberation which God brings to humanity in Christ.

PAUL'S KEY WORDS

Having described the effects of sin in the world, Paul now moves on to describe how the world has been touched by sin's opposite—"the justice that comes from faith" (4:13b). As Paul develops this theme of justification by faith, he uses several key words to describe the effects of Jesus' death and resurrection: *redemption*, *salvation*, *reconciliation* and, as we have already seen, *justification*.

Paul uses these various words not to suggest several contrasting realities but to point out the many-faceted nature of the one reality of Jesus' death and resurrection. Paul's writing of Romans could be compared to an artist holding up a precious jewel and turning it over and over in his hands so as to depict each view of the one jewel. Similarly, Paul turns the significance of Jesus' death and resurrection over and over in his mind and portrays for his reader different facets of the same reality.

'Redemption'

Redemption is an Old Testament concept going back to the Book of Leviticus (Lv). In Lv 25 the author describes the Israelite right to redeem certain indebted property. A modern example of redemption is the pawnshop system. A person who needs money can pawn a personal possession—let's say a watch—and receive money for it. If the person wants to get the watch back later, he or she can "redeem" it by paying the pawnbroker a fee within the allotted time. The person thus receives the watch back by way of "redemption."

In Old Testament times people could even "pawn" themselves if they became heavily indebted. Lv 25:47-55 prescribes certain rules by which a person sold into slavery for debt could be redeemed or liberated.

In applying the concept of redemption to Jesus' death and resurrection, Paul is saying that in Jesus God is now bringing humanity to the "plenteous redemption" (Psalm 130:7) foretold in the Old Testament. Thus, in Jesus, humanity attains its liberation from sin and becomes free.

Contrary to what we might expect, Paul does not call Jesus the "redeemer." Rather, he says that Jesus is "our redemption" (1 Cor 1:30). This is explained in Romans where Paul states, "All men are now undeservedly justified by the gift of God, through the redemption wrought in Christ Jesus" (3:24). Paul says that redemption is accomplished "in Christ Jesus" and not "by Christ Jesus" in order to emphasize that redemption is still continuing and that the final phase of the redemptive act will not be seen until Jesus' Parousia.

'Reconciliation'

Paul says that humanity is saved in Christ from "God's wrath" (5:9) and that humanity had once been "God's enemies" (5:10). By this Paul does not mean that God despised humanity and was waiting for the day when he could get even for the sins humanity had committed. This false understanding of "God's wrath" could lead to an equally false understanding of Jesus' death on the cross—namely, that God sadistically took out his anger against sinful humanity by making Jesus die on the cross.

By God's "wrath" Paul means God's repulsion at sin in the world, not God's hatred for sinners. Throughout the Old Testament Yahweh is said to be the "all-holy" in whose presence nothing unholy can come. Thus, anyone unholy is at such a distance from God as to experience him as not being present. In effect such a person may as well be God's enemy, for God's holiness constantly wars against unholiness in the same sense that light could be said to war with darkness. By reconciliation, therefore, Paul means not that God has lost his anger for those he hated—since God never had that anger in the first place—but that God's holiness has now overpowered humanity's unholiness.

'Salvation'

In Rom 5:9 Paul says that humanity will be "saved." Elsewhere in Romans he refers to "salvation" (1:16, 10:10, 13:11). What does he mean by "saved" and "salvation"? Paul sees salvation as the total consequence of God's action in history through Christ—past, present and future. As such, salvation encompasses the other effects of Jesus' death and resurrection we have been discussing: redemption, reconciliation and justification.

Salvation, however, is not simply a catchall term; it also has a nuance of meaning all its own. For Paul salvation refers primarily to the Endtime victory reserved by God for his redeemed creation. Salvation thus represents the sum total of God's action throughout time in making his creation free.

Like other Christians of his day, Paul had a changing awareness of when the final act of salvation—Jesus' Parousia—would take place. In his earlier letters Paul thought Jesus' Parousia would happen shortly, while in later letters his expectation of an imminent Parousia begins to wane. He thus speaks of the Endtime as already being here, yet still to come. In the same way he speaks of salvation as being fully realized and yet to come. (Compare 2 Cor 6:2 with Rom 5:9,10; 9:27; 10:9,13.) Perhaps the best way to reconcile Paul's "here-and-now" perspective on salvation with his "still-to-come" perspective is to contrast what he means by salvation with what he means by justification.

'Justification'

Paul more clearly understood justification to be the *now* result of Jesus' death and resurrection; he understood salvation to be the *Endtime* result. This becomes clearer upon reading Paul's words in Romans: *"Now* that we have been justified by his blood, it is all the more certain that we *shall* be saved by him from God's wrath" (5:9, emphases added). Thus, if a sidewalk preacher in Paul's day had asked him, "Have you been saved, Brother?" Paul would have perhaps replied, "I've been justified, Brother. My salvation is still taking place."

EFFECTS OF JUSTIFICATION

Now that we have clarified Paul's terminology, let us take up once again the progression of his thought in Romans. Having established that justification comes not through the Law but through faith, Paul moves into a discussion of the effects of justification on the Christian's daily life (6:1—8:39). Here we find the true significance of Romans to the second stage of New Testament development. We start to understand more deeply what intimacy with Jesus really means and how it is attained.

No Longer 'Slaves to Sin'

Paul says that justification by Christ means first that we are no longer "slaves to sin" (6:6). Consistent with his "already-here" and "still-to-come" mentality, Paul does not mean by this that we have completely eliminated the *tendency* toward sin which exists within us.

Keep in mind that for Paul sin is principally a *force* at work in the world and not just "bad behavior." This force has been defeated by Jesus but it takes time for the full effect of the opposing force—God's justice—to make itself completely visible. Thus, in the same breath with which Paul says we are "dead to sin" (6:11) he can say, "Do not...let sin rule your mortal body..." (6:12), indicating that our own efforts are still needed in the struggle against sin.

Death to the Law

A second effect of Christians' justification is their death to the Law (7:4). When Paul says, "Now we have been released from the law..." (7:6), he is stretching the connotation of *law* to refer principally to the human-made religious practices which had grown out of the first five books of the Old Testament. In other words he is not saying, "Throw out the Ten Commandments," but that Christians are freed from the false doctrine which holds that religious forms and rituals make one pleasing to God. Having established this point, Paul immediately returns to a more restrictive usage of *law* in the sense of the code given by God to Moses (7:7,8,12). This Law is "holy and just and good" (7:12), since it clearly exposes sin for what it is.

Empowerment for Holiness

Yet people have no inherent power within themselves to keep this Law (7:18b). They do not do the good they will to do but the evil which they do not intend (7:19). Humanity's powerlessness to keep the Law is overcome by "God, through Jesus Christ our Lord" (7:25), who empowers the Christian to bring external conduct into consistency with one's inner desire to keep God's Law (7:22). A third effect of justification, then, is empowerment for holiness.

Indwelling of the Spirit

A fourth effect is the presence of the Spirit in a Christian's life. Essentially what the Spirit does is to effectuate and authenticate the Christian's adoption as God's child:

> All who are led by the Spirit of God are sons of God....The Spirit himself gives witness with our spirit that we are children of God.
> (Rom 8:14,16)

In typical fashion Paul does not portray the Spirit's action as an instantaneous and overwhelming replacement of a person's faculties by God's unlimited power. For Paul, human freedom is always depicted as a divine/human partnership in which the human partner remains free to accept God's power or to reject it. Consequently, Paul stresses that God's release of his Spirit in the human spirit does not immediately eliminate the weakness resulting from sin's action.

The indwelling of God's Spirit in the human person is thus said by Paul to be *"first* fruits" (8:23); that is, the Spirit has *begun* its work of bringing the human person to total freedom in God, but there is still work to be done. For that reason Christians find that, even though they have received the gift of the Spirit, they still "groan inwardly while [they] await the redemption of [their] bodies" (8:23).

The Spirit, however, helps the Christian in his or her weakness. The Spirit empowers the Christian to claim adoption by God, enabling him or her to call God "'Abba!' (that is, 'Father')" (8:15). This spontaneous response to the Spirit's work is an essential step in the process of growing from infatuation to intimacy and thus to liberation in Christ. For one cannot be that which one has experienced but not proclaimed.

For example, an orphan who is adopted and moves into his new home might proudly tell his friends as he points to his adoptive father, "That's my daddy!" The boy's proclamation of his sonship verifies and authenticates his change of status. Without that proclamation his change of status is not yet real in his life.

In the same way, until Christians announce their change of status in Christ by proclaiming their "sonship," then that sonship is not yet real. Paul shows that it is the Spirit who effectuates the Christian's change of status; the Spirit puts into the Christian's heart the awareness of God as "Abba," and releases within the Christian the power to proclaim God as "Father."

The Spirit further helps Christians in their weakness by interceding to the Father from within the depths of their own spirits:

The Spirit too helps us in our weakness, for we do not know how to pray as we ought; but the Spirit himself makes intercession for us with groanings that cannot be expressed in speech. He who searches hearts knows what the Spirit means, for the Spirit intercedes for the saints as God himself wills. (Rom 8:26-27)

The image Paul suggests here is an amazing one—God himself praying within the Christian's heart so that the prayer will unerringly achieve God's purpose. So much does the Father love his children, Paul is saying, that he not only grants their needs but expresses those needs!

Thus, God's entire purpose in releasing the Spirit within his children is to transform them into God's own holiness. Paul refers to this final goal of God's transforming work as "the glory to be revealed in us" (8:18). Astonishingly, not only will God's human children eventually share in his glory, but the rest of creation also: "...the world itself will be freed from its slavery to corruption and share in the glorious freedom of the children of God" (8:21).

By Jesus' death and resurrection, then, *all* of God's creation has been invigorated by the Spirit and pointed in the direction of ultimate transformation by God into his own glory. Given these amazing realities, what is there left to say? Paul's answer is, "If God is for us, who can be against us?" (8:31).

RESPONSIBILITIES OF CHRISTIAN FREEDOM

Paul's understanding of freedom as "freedom *for*" necessitated his walking long, lonely miles through a desert of sacrifice and selfless service. He now prepares his readers for the sacrifices *they* must make as they live their Christian freedom in the world.

He succinctly states the responsibilities of this freedom as he calls upon his readers "to offer your bodies as a living sacrifice holy and acceptable to God..." (12:1). In order to make the sacrifices required by the Christian life, Paul's readers must "be transformed by the renewal of your mind..." (12:2).

For Paul, the mind is the starting point of the Christian's day-to-day participation in the ongoing process of God's liberation. For that reason Christians must closely guard what is admitted into their minds. In Philippians Paul had said, "...your thoughts should be wholly directed to all that is true, all that deserves respect, all that is honest, pure, admirable, decent, virtuous, or worthy of praise" (Phil 4:8).

Mental transformation is important for Paul because thinking and planning are the basis of activity. A person who tries to carry out the demands of Christian life without first having transformed his or her mind may be likened to "the man who built his house on the ground without any foundation. When the torrent rushed upon it, it immediately fell in and was completely destroyed" (Lk 6:49). Like Luke, Paul knew that "each man speaks from his heart's abundance" (Lk 6:45b)—"heart," or *kardia* in Greek, being virtually identical in Paul's thought with *nous*, or "mind."

After his advice about renewing one's mind, Paul moves on to list some of the attitudes and actions which are to characterize Christian life:

> Anticipate each other in showing respect...persevere in prayer...be generous in offering hospitality...bless your persecutors...never repay injury with injury...live peaceably with everyone...obey the authorities...pay taxes...owe no debt to anyone...live honorably as in daylight; not in carousing and drunkenness, not in sexual excess and lust, not in quarreling and jealousy.
> (Rom 12:10b,12,13b,14,17a,18;13:1,6,8,13)

The sum of these actions is contained in the Scripture verse "Love your neighbor as yourself" (Lv 19:18b; Rom 13:9). As in his Corinthian correspondence, Paul once again underscores the primacy of love in the Christian life. Thus, when we say that for Paul freedom is "freedom *for*," the most Pauline completion we could make for that phrase would be "freedom for *love*."

In essence what Paul sees God doing in a person's life is transforming that person more and more into a lover—a lover like Christ, who "while we were still sinners...died for us" (5:8). Paul concludes his treatise on Christian freedom by urging his readers to remain ever free to love, so that they may take to others the fruits of love won for them on the cross.

In Romans Paul has given us a new perspective on the transformation from infatuation to intimacy. Based on freedom, our maturing relationship with Jesus produces God's own life—his own power—within us. Perhaps now we can see more clearly how essential Romans is to an understanding of Jesus' earthly accomplishment, and how a deepened appreciation of that accomplishment draws Christians into an ever more intimate relationship with Jesus.

CHAPTER SIX

LIVING THE NEW WAY

**1 and 2 Timothy, Titus, James,
1 and 2 Peter, Jude, Philemon**

Paul was not the only New Testament letter writer. In this chapter we will consider other Christian letter writers and their works, specifically the non-Pauline letters 1 and 2 Timothy (Tm), Titus (Ti), James (Jas), 1 and 2 Peter (Pt) and Jude. Lastly, we will consider an authentically Pauline letter, Philemon (Phlm).

With the exception of Philemon, all the letters we will consider in this chapter have several features in common: Each purports to be written by an apostle or some other famous early Christian leader but, in actuality, was written by someone whose name we don't know. Each purports to be written during the lifetime of the person said to be the author but, for the most part, was written well after his time. Each of these writings concerns itself not with a newly founded missionary Church, but a Church that is gradually asserting its own stable identity within its environment.

Consequently, the concern of these letters is not to explain the rudiments of Christian doctrine. They detail how people who already understand that doctrine are to put it into practice—usually in a setting hostile to the Christian message.

These writings give us yet another perspective on the second stage of New Testament development. They show how to live a life of intimacy with Jesus in a society where a more mature and organized Church is looked upon either with suspicion or with outright hostility. As we shall see, perseverance in the face of rejection by the world is a subtle undertone of these letters.

69

These letters—perhaps better than any we have considered thus far—show that intimacy with Jesus is not an individual matter. Such a relationship involves intimacy with others as well, and we find in 1 and 2 Timothy and Titus that the "others" Christians are called to love live with them in a growing Church that is becoming more and more institutionalized.

CHARISMATIC VS. INSTITUTIONAL?

It is tempting to label the New Testament works we have previously discussed as "charismatic" and the works we will consider in this chapter as "institutional." Such a dichotomy would suggest that the first category of writings was composed by fiery evangelists writing out of their immediate experience of God's power in their lives, while the second category was written by stuffy Church bureaucrats trying to maintain the status quo and preserve their own ecclesiastical interests.

Such a characterization would drastically miss the mark. Both sets of writings are authentically second-stage in that they both concern themselves with the Christian's call to be intimate with Jesus. Yet they do this in different ways. While it is true that the writings we will consider in this chapter lack the verve and dynamism of their predecessors, it is *not* true that the Churches addressed by these writings were Spirit-less institutions, untouched by a life-changing, intimate love affair with Jesus.

The Churches addressed by these writings were struggling to make the life of the Spirit real amidst problems which the firebrand evangelists of the 50's and 60's had not had to face: how the Church grows and maintains itself in the workaday world; what type of system the Church should adopt for appointing apostolic successors and other leaders; how the Church addresses the growing division among Christians over certain aspects of the apostolic teachings; how it responds to assertions by nonbelievers that an organized Christianity is opposed to earthly governments; and, finally, how the Church decides which aspects of doctrine should be incorporated into its "official" body of beliefs and which should not.

We should keep in mind that the changing conditions of the world in which the readers of these letters lived called for changing responses to the one gospel truth they had inherited. They sought to apply the freedom won for them by Jesus to new situations which threatened that freedom. We will see what these new situations were as we discuss each writing in more detail. Let us begin our study with the Pastorals.

Who Wrote 1 and 2 Timothy and Titus?

Let us begin by explaining what it means to say that the so-called Pastoral Letters (that is, 1 and 2 Timothy and Titus) are "non-Pauline." We know that Paul was sent to Rome by the Roman procurator Porcius Festus about the year 60. In order to have written 1 and 2 Timothy and Titus, Paul would have had to have left Rome, returned to the East, gone back to Rome a second time and been imprisoned a second time. That at least is the conclusion suggested by internal evidence in these three letters. Yet there is no other evidence—scriptural or traditional—that Paul left Rome, made a trip east and returned to Rome a second time.

Furthermore, the subject matter of 1 and 2 Timothy and Titus is pastoral advice—how Christians are to run the day-to-day affairs of their local Churches and how they are to respond to the normal problems facing a growing organization. (Thus these epistles are called the "Pastoral Letters.") It is unlikely, however, that Paul, fresh out of prison in Rome and fully aware of the crisis facing the Roman Church during the mid-60's, would have concentrated on such themes. And surely there would have been a little more of Paul's old fire.

Because of such considerations, most Scripture scholars conclude that 1 and 2 Timothy and Titus were written several years after Paul's death by an anonymous author who borrowed Paul's name and the content of his teaching. The writer of the Pastorals did this in order to suggest that his teaching was as worthy of acceptance as if Paul himself had written it. This was a common literary convention in ancient times.

The Pastorals' Message

These letters could be collectively subtitled "Sound Doctrine." One of the author's overriding concerns is to delineate for his readers those aspects of Christian doctrine which are authentic, as opposed to certain false teachings circulating at the time. (See 1 Tm 1:10; 4:6; 6:3; 2 Tm 4:3; Ti 1:9; 2:1.) They are more interested in *preserving* the Christian teaching for believers than they are in *explaining* that teaching to unbelievers.

The Pastorals refute the false teaching that Christianity is incompatible with ordinary life in the world. For that reason, these letters employ language which may appear to us somewhat conservative. The Church is referred to as "the pillar and bulwark of truth" (1 Tm 3:15). Authentic Christian doctrines are spoken of as "the teaching

proper to true religion" (1 Tm 6:3). The personal qualities of bishops
(1 Tm 3:2-5) and of presbyters (Ti 1:6) remind us of the wording on
plaques awarded at Chamber of Commerce banquets. (It is doubtful
that the "wild and insubordinate" Paul—Ti 1:6—would ever have
qualified as the reputable city-father type praised by the Pastorals.)

We should not, however, read our experience of history back
into the Pastorals and condemn them for being ecclesiastically
chauvinistic. For us the phrase "true religion" conjures up stern-faced
Spanish Inquisitors or latter-day fundamentalists certain that their way
is the *only* right way. "Bulwark of truth" suggests the huge fortress-like
medieval cathedrals and monasteries which stood as bastions against
the inroads of heresy. The civic virtues that bishops, elders and deacons
are to emulate call to mind pudgy old clerics sipping tea in mansions
filled with dutiful house servants.

In actuality these images would have clashed severely with the
reality of the Christians' world during the time the Pastorals were
written. The wording in these letters describes not a Church
triumphalistically asserting its power and authority over those who
disagreed with it, but a Church seeking to survive and find its place in
a world largely opposed to its beliefs. Thus the Pastorals can be excused
for their periodic lapses into somewhat conservative language. (Perhaps
*pre*servative language is a more accurate description.)

Church Order

It was the Pastorals' concern for strengthening the tender shoot
of developing Christianity which led them to stress order and discipline.
They were written during a time when the apostles and other original
leaders of the Church had either died or were dying. The question was
how to select new leaders and what type of duties these leaders should
have in an increasingly organized Church.

For that reason the letters are ostensibly addressed to Timothy
and Titus, two of Paul's handpicked disciples appointed by him to be
elders-in-chief of, respectively, the Church at Ephesus and the Church
in Crete. It is doubtful, however, that Timothy and Titus were alive at
the time the Pastorals were written. Their names are used in these letters
to standardize the advice that the author wanted to give to all Christian
leaders and, through these leaders, to all the members of "God's
household" (1 Tm 3:15).

The titles which the author assigns to the various Church leaders
are "bishop" (1 Tm 3:2; Ti 1:7), "presbyter" (1 Tm 4:14; 5:17,19; Ti
1:6) and "deacon" (1 Tm 3:8,10,12). These titles do not correspond
exactly to the hierarchy of our own day. The "bishop" of the Pastorals

connotes "elder," while "presbyter" and "deacon" are used in the sense of "assistant." More than likely there was more than one bishop or elder in a given community.

The duties of "bishops" and of their assistants varied from community to community. There was no standardized definition of ministerial duties at the time the Pastorals were written.

Yet certain duties were preeminent, especially preaching and teaching. It is clear from the Pastorals that both elders and assistants were qualified to perform these functions (1 Tm 4:13; 5:17).

While there were undoubtedly many part-time volunteer elders and assistants, there were also professional elders and presbyters who, according to the author of 1 Timothy, "deserve to be paid double" (5:17). And the Pastoral Letters also reveal that in each local Church there was one man who was regarded as the chief authority. In time the word *bishop* came to be reserved for this man; whether it was so used at the time of the Pastorals is unclear.

The Pastorals teach that the elders and their assistants—the combined body of Church leaders—are to shepherd a flock that is orderly, virtuous and disciplined. This is the "kind of conduct [which] befits a member of God's household" (1 Tm 3:15). To define this conduct is one of the chief reasons the Pastorals were written (1 Tm 3:14-15).

Church leaders should inspire proper conduct not by authoritarian decree but by their own example (1 Tm 4:15-16). Then like the elders and their assistants, the rest of the Church must be "serious, straightforward, and truthful. They may not overindulge in drink..." (1 Tm 3:8); they are to "turn from youthful passions and pursue integrity, faith, love and peace..." (2 Tm 2:22); and each of them should be "hospitable and a lover of goodness; steady, just, holy, and self-controlled" (Ti 1:8).

Lest these qualities suggest to us a Christianity that has forgotten Paul's stirring words about Christian freedom, we should remember that Paul himself also counseled self-control, discipline and restraint. Paul and the Pastoral writers show us that both freedom and responsibility are essential elements of the Christian life-style.

OTHER LETTER WRITERS

James
In the introduction to James the author identifies himself as "James, a servant of God and of the Lord Jesus Christ" (Jas 1:1). Who is this James? There are only three candidates. The first is James, son

of Zebedee, apostle and brother of John. This James cannot be the author of our letter, since he was beheaded by Herod (Acts 12:1) no later than the year 47 A.D. and it is obvious that James was written well after that year.

A second candidate is James, son of Alphaeus, also an apostle, and otherwise known as "James the Lesser." Yet we know nothing about this James other than that he appears in the Synoptic lists of apostles and in Acts 1:13. It is doubtful that such a hidden figure ever became a well-known evangelist, or that later Christians would have remembered him as being of such significance that they would have attached his name to an important document.

The final possibility for the letter's author is James, "the brother of the Lord" (Gal 1:19). In actuality, it is this James whose name is used in Jas 1:1. Who was this "brother of the Lord," and did he actually write the letter which was attributed to him?

We know from the Gospels that, except for Jesus' mother, the members of Jesus' family did not think well of his ministry. At one point they considered Jesus to be "out of his mind" (Mk 3:21). Nowhere in the Gospels do any of his relatives—other than Mary—put any faith in him. Thus, the James referred to in Jas 1:1 probably came to believe in Jesus as Messiah and Lord—like most other people—only after Jesus' death.

Was James Jesus' "brother" in the sense of being a child of Mary? Based on Scripture we cannot answer that question one way or another. Scriptural and other evidence, however, would tend to support a negative answer, for several reasons.

Jews in Jesus' time meant more by the concept of family than we do. "Family" included not only mother, father, sister and brother, but also uncles, aunts, cousins, grandparents, etc. The Jews, like other ancient peoples, thought of family as the extended family. Consistent with this, they had no word in their language for "cousin" except the same word which they used for "brother."

If Jesus had cousins named James, Joses, Judas and Simon (Mk 6:3), he would have called each of these cousins "brother" (in Greek, *adelphos*). Jesus' usage of "brother" to describe his cousins would have been followed by both the Synoptic writers and Paul.

This conclusion is not contradicted by Luke's reference to Jesus as Mary's "first-born son" (Lk 2:7). The term Luke uses here is a technical one, indicating certain rights and responsibilities Jesus had under the Jewish Law. So when Luke uses "first-born," he does not necessarily mean that there was also a "second-born."

When these and other details* surrounding the Jewish

74

understanding of "brother" and "family" are considered along with the early Church's traditional belief in Mary's perpetual virginity, our conclusion is that James, "the brother of the Lord," was probably Jesus' first cousin.

Not only did James come to accept Jesus as Lord, he also became a highly respected leader in the early Church—rivaling Peter himself in importance (see Acts 15). As Peter turned more and more to missionary endeavors which took him out of Jerusalem, James supplanted Peter as chief elder of Jerusalem. This is remarkable given the fact that James had not been an apostle.

It is possible that after his resurrection Jesus appeared to James (1 Cor 15:7—we don't know for sure which James is meant in this verse), and that during this appearance Jesus commissioned James to some great work—just as Jesus had done when he appeared to Paul. At any rate—whatever the actual facts of James's early Christian life—it is clear that by the late 40's of the first century James was thought of as a pillar of the Church.

Did James write the letter ascribed to him? We don't know. As with the Pastorals, the author of James was possibly someone who used James's name and reputation in order to promote the teaching of the letter. The author's audience is composed principally of Jewish Christians living within Palestine. Notice that the author specifically addresses himself to the concerns of this group, such as how they were to conduct themselves in the synagogue (Jas 2:2). (At this time the Jewish Christians were still using synagogues for their meeting places.)

James is not really a letter in the ordinary sense, even though its opening verse purports to be the first lines of a letter. In actuality it is a distinct style of writing popular in New Testament times called *exhortation*. In an exhortation the writer is trying to motivate his readers to a certain type of conduct. Like an orator, the author of James is less interested in teaching fine points of theology than in persuading his audience to take a certain course of action.

The action which James encourages may be summarized as follows: to demonstrate your faith by your deeds of loving service, and to persevere in your hope for salvation.

A key teaching of James is found in 2:14-26 where the author discusses faith and good works. This section has generated much commentary because of an apparent contradiction between James and

---

*In the Greek version of the Old Testament, for example, *adelphos* was frequently used by the Jewish translators to refer to someone who was obviously *not* another's biological brother.

the letters of Paul. The verse cited by those who see a conflict is Jas 2:24: "You must perceive that a person is justified by his works and not by faith alone."

In reality there is no conflict between Paul and the author of James. As we have already established, Paul certainly does not teach a gospel of faith without works (*works* being defined here as acts of loving service and self-sacrifice). By the same token, the author of James does not teach a gospel of works without faith. Each man looks at faith/works as a continuum of inner belief and outer expression of that belief. Paul expresses his understanding of that continuum from one perspective, and the author of James from another.

For both Paul and the author of James, faith is the foundation—the substratum underlying one's works—while works are the results of faith, results which not only *signify* but *effectuate* faith and make it real. The author of James challenges the reader to "show me your faith without works, and I will show you the faith that underlies my works!" (Jas 2:18b). In other words, he is saying, "You can't demonstrate that you have faith unless you perform the works which are motivated by faith." For faith in a vacuum is no faith at all. James speaks loudly and clearly, then, to all those who would make Christianity a private affair between themselves and God.

According to James, Christianity is not simply a religion of belief; it is also a religion of action. We would quite likely be very uncomfortable to have the author preach in our churches today. He might say to us, "All right, folks, once the singing is finished we'll meet in the poor section of town for a day of Christian service." Would some of us perhaps protest, "But, sir, we can't do that. We're too busy practicing our faith"? Are we perhaps only infatuated with Jesus and unwilling to become intimate with him as challenged by the author of James?

1 Peter

The First Letter of Peter is similar in many respects to the Pastorals. It stresses "obedience to the truth" (1:22) and respect for "every human institution" (2:13). Like the Pastorals it is concerned with showing that Christianity is no threat to civil society and that one's Christianity is compatible with one's citizenship. Also like the Pastorals, 1 Peter teaches that Christian virtue practiced openly will silence fears and criticisms of nonbelievers: "You must silence the ignorant talk of foolish men by your good behavior" (2:15b).

Unlike the Pastorals, 1 Peter is more of an exhortation—such as James—than a true letter. Like James, it is written in the name of a famous and respected Christian leader in order to urge Christians authoritatively to live the gospel openly and constantly. Also, like James it is concerned with the theme of perseverance. The author of 1 Peter teaches perseverance not only in the sense of hope for final reward (though this too is taught, for example, in 1:13b), but also in the sense of steadfastness in the face of persecution. The author of 1 Peter does not identify any particular group of persecutors. Perhaps he is referring simply to the general atmosphere of tension and even open hostility which Christians faced in the secular society during the late first century.

Jude, 2 Peter

These two letters were likewise written by unknown writers and ascribed to respected elders of the early Church—in this case, Peter, whom we know well, and Jude, who was probably another of Jesus' cousins (Mk 6:3—called "Judas" in modern translations).

Like the Pastorals, Jude and 2 Peter are each concerned with promoting "sound doctrine" in opposition to the heretical teachings prominent in the late first century. The author of Jude characterizes the basic collection of Christian beliefs as "the faith delivered once for all to the saints" (Jude 1:3b).

Parts of 2 Peter rely heavily on Jude (compare Jude 4-13 and 2 Peter 2:1-18). Most scholars question the author's originality and think that 2 Peter is by and large a copy of verses found in Jude and elsewhere. The author of 2 Peter was obviously familiar with other Christian writings. He knew Paul's letters (2 Pt 3:15-16), and he was familiar with written accounts of Jesus' transfiguration (2 Pt 1:15-17), perhaps having read these accounts in early Gospel manuscripts. He also refers to 1 Peter (2 Pt 3:1).

The author of 2 Peter addresses a heresy which denied Christ's Second Coming. By the late first century, Christians could obviously no longer look forward to Jesus' "immediate" return, as some of their predecessors had done. Some people pointed to this nonfulfillment of a prominent early Christian belief to discredit Christianity in its entirety.

The author reminds his readers that God's conception of time is not humanity's conception. Measured by God's standard, Jesus may indeed return "soon": "In the Lord's eyes, one day is as a thousand years and a thousand years are as a day" (2 Pt 3:8). The author suggests that the timing of the Last Judgment is unimportant; what is important is the spiritual condition in which Christians will find themselves on the last day. For that reason Christians should use the time before the last day to attend to their salvation (2 Pt 3:9-10).

Philemon

The final work we will consider in this chapter is a note which Paul wrote about the year 62 to a wealthy young Colossian named Philemon. (We at last return to a work which everyone admits is exactly what it purports to be!) This letter represents Paul's personal plea—which becomes more like a command as the letter progresses—for Philemon to accept back in a spirit of Christian love his runaway slave, Onesimus.

Onesimus had somehow made his way to Rome, where Paul met him and converted him to Christianity. Perhaps Onesimus was serving a jail sentence for some petty crime in the same Roman prison where Paul was confined. At any rate, Paul returned Onesimus to Philemon "confident" (Phlm 21) that Philemon would welcome his slave back as he would welcome Paul himself (17).

Nothing could more vividly dramatize the life-changing effect of a person's conversion to Christianity than for a master to take back under his roof a runaway slave—and not just to take him back but to accept him as a "beloved brother" (16). Philemon was challenged by Paul to demonstrate his desire for deeper intimacy with Jesus in a very practical and painful way.

Thomas Merton once said that "people who don't act on their beliefs don't really have those beliefs." Paul gave Philemon a challenge every Christian must face—to show that the gospel is indeed real in his or her life. Paul constantly affirms that Christianity is much more than assent to a doctrine; it is a response to a personal call from the resurrected Lord to "love your neighbor as yourself" (see Rom 13:9b).

ON TO THE THIRD STAGE

This concludes our discussion of the books belonging to the second stage of New Testament development. It is now time to turn to the books of the third stage.

The third stage of New Testament writings represents the final step in the Christian's growth process: the transformation from self to Christ. Paul expresses this transformation succinctly when he says, "...the life I live now is not my own; Christ is living in me" (Gal 2:20). We characterize these writings as an expression of the Christian's *identification* with Jesus—similar to the third stage in any maturing love relationship. The writings in this third stage are Colossians (Col),

Ephesians (Eph), Hebrews (Heb) and the works associated with the apostle John (Jn).

Just as long-married couples express themselves through nuances and subtleties of thought which escape the attention of the casual observer, writers of the third stage of New Testament development likewise use language that is frequently beyond ordinary understanding. This is because these writers are writing not so much from their own perspective as from the perspective of their beloved.

To understand the third-stage writings, then, we must enter as best we can into that deep union between lover and beloved which characterizes these writings. We must—more so than we did with the writings of the first and second stages—allow our minds to transcend ordinary categories of thought and perception, so that we can begin to appreciate the inner life of union with Christ experienced by the writers of the third stage. As we pass from the second to the third stage of New Testament development, we enter new spiritual territory.

CHAPTER SEVEN

'THE MYSTERY OF CHRIST IN YOU'

Colossians, Ephesians

The aging soldier pulled his wool cloak more tightly around his shoulders. A damp February wind was blowing across the Tiber toward the former palace which the soldier had been appointed to run as a prison. Most of his wards were highly educated people, learned in fields of knowledge with which the soldier had never come into contact. Within his prison were runaway Greek slaves who had tutored princes; magicians and sorcerers from the Orient; kings who had been the victims of plots and coups in faraway fiefdoms of the Empire.

The soldier regarded old Lucius' converted palace not as a prison but as a university. Thanks to his 10 years of service there, the soldier could now converse adequately in several languages and had learned to read and write Latin and Greek. He was familiar with the teachings of Plato and Aristotle. He knew of the Brahmin of the Hindus and the mysterious Yahweh of the Jews.

Over a year ago a Jewish prisoner had arrived from Jerusalem. True to Jewish form, he was an enigma of a man: a Roman citizen; a rabbi; the victim of a plot by the Jewish elite in Palestine; and an alleged heretic and blasphemer for believing that God manifested himself in the form of a certain Jesus.

After the soldier had settled the new arrival in his quarters, he hinted that, should the Jew make himself available for teaching and discussion, certain liberties and conveniences could be arranged. The Jew responded to the soldier's overture by telling him that while awaiting trial he planned to spread the "good news" of Jesus to the other Jews

81

in Rome and to anyone else who would listen.

During the next few months the Jew spoke openly and often about the "new way of God's Kingdom" and about Jesus as the Jews' Messiah. Some of the Jews whom the soldier brought to the prison considered the inmate-evangelist a dangerous heretic and defiler of the truth. Others accepted his teachings and returned often to hear the man preach the "good news of Jesus, the Lord and Christ."

One of those who accepted the prisoner's teaching was the soldier himself. The Jew was amazed at the depth of the soldier's intuition and understanding. The soldier's probing questions matched the Jew's thought step for step.

On one occasion the soldier said to the Jew: "Master, you have taught us well about our new life in Christ. You have said that our Baptism has made us 'new creatures,' participants in the risen life of our resurrected Lord. You have said that through his Spirit living in us we die to ourselves and come to life in Christ Jesus. Is this not correct?"

"Yes, my friend, you have understood well what I have said," the Jew responded.

"It puzzles me, Master, how you can say that the more we die to ourselves the freer we become. If Christ indeed takes over our lives do we not somehow become captives of Christ? Do we not lose our own freedom to think, to act and to choose?"

"That is the great beauty of the mystery of 'Christ in you,' my friend. Christ alone is true freedom, and thus whatever freedom we imagine we have now is nothing compared to the freedom we will ultimately gain by surrendering ourselves to the divine Self within us. Transformation into Christ is never a loss, though it may seem that at times. It is always gain. The more we die to ourselves the more alive we become in Christ. To become fully yourself means to allow God to be fully divine within you.

"Perhaps something I have just written will help you understand this better, my friend. Will you please read it before our next meeting and give me your thoughts?"

PAUL THE SPIRITUAL MASTER

The scene just imagined suggests a picture of Paul which is perhaps foreign to us—that of Paul as a master of the spiritual life. We ordinarily get the picture of him as a preacher, pastor or evangelist. Rarely do we think of him as a person of great spiritual awareness—a mystic, if you will—such as Teresa of Avila or John of the Cross. Yet Paul *was* a great mystic; he was a person continuously aware in the depth of his being of the indwelling presence of God.

In this chapter we will consider Colossians (Col) and Ephesians (Eph), writings which could only have been penned by a mystic—that is, someone who is constantly aware of God through personal experience, not simply theoretical knowledge.

The Paul imprisoned in Rome (c.61-63 A.D.) was a man who had grown greatly in spiritual insight and awareness. He was a far different Paul than the man who first took to the evangelistic trail about the year 50 A.D. During those intervening years his relationship to the Christ who had broken into his life on the road to Damascus had deepened and matured.

It is the mature Paul's awareness of Christ which we find reflected in Colossians and Ephesians. In these two works we discover the insights of someone who has obviously gone well beyond infatuation with Jesus, and even beyond intimacy. Paul has reached a new level of awareness of the risen Christ—the level of *identification* with him.

Another name we could give to this level of awareness is *Christ-consciousness*, the ability to look upon reality with the same perception as Christ himself. In the third stage of the ever-deepening love relationship with Jesus, one leaves behind not only one's values and desires, but even the very perceptual framework under which one has previously operated. One literally develops a new state of consciousness, a means of perception entirely similar to that of Christ himself.

With Colossians and Ephesians, we begin a discussion of the first of the works typifying this third stage of Christian growth: *identification with Christ*.

WHO WROTE COLOSSIANS?

Some Scripture scholars think Colossians was not actually written by Paul but, like the Pastorals, by a later writer using Paul's name. They base their conclusion on the differences in vocabulary, style and thought between Colossians and the universally accepted Pauline letters. For example, scholars have isolated about 50 theological terms in Colossians which do not appear in Paul's earlier letters.

Furthermore, there is a distinction between the understanding of eschatology found in Colossians and that in Pauline works such as 1 Thessalonians or 1 Corinthians. In Colossians the writer exhibits scarcely a trace of the future-oriented eschatology of such passages as Rom 6:4-5. Rather, the author sees the Christian as sharing fully in God's resurrection power *now* (e.g., Col 2:12).

Scholars who conclude that Colossians was actually written by Paul see the difference in vocabulary as Paul's response to certain errors which he wanted to refute. Thus he adopted some of the very language used in heretical doctrines in order to stress the superiority of his teachings.

For example, Paul used the Greek word *pleroma* (meaning "fullness"—Col 1:19, 2:9) in order to counteract the erroneous teaching that lesser spiritual beings each contributed their share to God's being in such a way that "absolute fullness" would mean the sum total of all these other beings. According to this heresy, these other beings would be necessary intermediaries between humanity and God. Colossians makes it clear that God's fullness (*pleroma*) resides only in Christ, and that he alone is intermediary between humanity and God (Col 1:19).

Scholars who support the Pauline authenticity of Colossians see the difference in theology between this letter and Paul's earlier ones to be an indication of the development of Paul's thought, not an indication of a different writer. They would say, for example, that Paul in Colossians looks upon the Christian's resurrected life more as a present than a future experience because Paul himself had come to experience a fuller reality of God's resurrection power in his own life.

While there is merit to both positions, the evidence challenging the authenticity of Colossians is inconclusive. Thus, even though there is some doubt as to the Pauline authorship, we will adhere to the position generally advanced by the "pro-Pauline" scholars: that it was written by the apostle Paul while he was imprisoned in Rome during the years 61-63 in order to combat various errors which had arisen since the time the Colossian Church was founded.

THE MESSAGE OF COLOSSIANS

One of Paul's principal concerns in Colossians is to refute the belief that the world is ruled by spiritual beings of a lesser order than God. These are generically labeled "angels" (Col 2:18) and sub-categorized as "thrones or dominations, principalities or powers" (1:16). The erroneous belief about these angels was connected with certain *gnostic* teachings.

Gnosticism divides the world into two realms: matter, which is evil, and spirit, which is good. Gnostic teachers purportedly showed others how to escape from the imprisonment of corrupt matter into the realm of pure spirit by revealing a secret "gnosis," or knowledge, to their disciples. This gnosis was given only to those sufficiently purified, either in this life or in previous incarnations.

Paul refutes these gnostic teachings by writing of Christ's divine preexistence and, thus, his superiority to all created spirits such as angels. Paul writes: Christ is "the image of the invisible God" (Col 1:15).

Paul expands this thought by saying that "in him [Christ] everything in heaven and on earth was created, things visible and invisible..." (Col 1:16). Obviously, if all of these things were created "in Christ" then Christ is superior to them, and this is a major point Paul wants to establish.

For Paul the preexistent Christ is the principle and means of creation; that is, he is the "substance" in which all created things subsist and the seed from which all creation springs. Paul believes that creation takes place not only *in* Christ but also *through* him (Col 1:16) and *for* him—that is, Christ is the end or fulfillment of creation.

One way to explain Paul's teaching that creation is "in, through and for" Christ is to say that he is the *source*, *course* and *goal* of all creation: *source*, in that all creation comes from him; *course*, in that all creation is constantly maintained in being by him (Col 1:17); and *goal*, in that all creation is called to return to Christ in glorified form. Paul says:

> When, finally, all has been subjected to the Son, he will then subject himself to the One who made all things subject to him, so that God may be all in all. (1 Cor 15:28)

The Body of Christ

After establishing Christ as superior to all created beings, Paul relates Christ's primacy to the Church: "It is he [Christ] who is head of the body, the church..." (Col 1:18). This is the first time in Paul's writings that he equates the Church with Christ's body. Previously when Paul said, "You, then, are the body of Christ" (1 Cor 12:27), he was using a metaphor to express the *moral* union of all Christians working together toward the same goal. In Colossians, however, Paul sees the Church as Christ's body in a deeper sense.

In Colossians (and in Ephesians) Paul understands the Church to be the place where the resurrected Christ lives in the world. Not only *should* the Church be one in Christ (1 Cor 12:27), the Church actually *is* one in Christ. According to Colossians, then, the Church's oneness with Christ is a metaphysical (not just metaphorical) reality, and this is so whether the Church's actions bespeak this oneness or not.

The degree to which the Church actually demonstrates its true nature as the body of Christ depends upon the individual members of the Church growing in their relationship with Christ from infatuation

85

to intimacy to identification. The Church as a whole cannot be fully identified with Christ unless the individual members of the Church are identified with him.

Identification With Christ

Paul emphasizes this thought in his own way by urging the Colossians to become "perfect" (4:12) and "complete in Christ" (1:28). He prays that the Colossians will attain "full knowledge" and "perfect wisdom" (1:9). He obviously saw Christian life as one of evolving spiritual consciousness, a continually expanding awareness of the reality of Christ living within oneself and within others. For Paul, the goal of Christian life on earth was nothing less than a manifestation of one's share in the "fullness of deity" (Col 2:9) which resides in Christ.

According to Paul, Christians achieve their growth toward union with God through identification with Christ, the "head" of the body into which all Christians are integrated. Paul says that Christ is "head of the body, the church" (1:18). Further, Paul says that Christ the head should be looked upon as the "source" from which the body draws its support and through which it achieves its growth (2:19). (In ancient times people thought that the head was the energy source from which the organs of the body were controlled and empowered.) Paul saw the body (Church) as being called to grow into more and more coordination with the head or, as he put it, into "the full maturity of Christ the head" (Eph 4:15).

The means by which Christians become more and more *identified* with Christ the head is by filling up in their own bodies "what is lacking in the sufferings of Christ" (Col 1:24). Paul does not mean that Christ's suffering and death on the cross did not fully accomplish the salvation of humanity. Rather, the redemption of all creation—which still "groans" (Rom 8:22) as it awaits ultimate fulfillment—is an ongoing process, initiated by Jesus but completed by the Church. Once the Church has "filled up," that is, completed its mission of suffering, then redemption will have reached full term and history will end.

The sufferings which the Christian must endure are those which come from living and spreading the gospel in a world often hostile to this message. The Christian, then, "suffers" as he or she participates in the mission of making disciples of all nations (Mt 28:19). For Paul, the path to identification with Christ follows in Jesus' own footsteps of selfless service on behalf of the gospel.

WHO WROTE EPHESIANS?

Ephesians, like Colossians, exhibits characteristics which

suggest non-Pauline authorship. For example, in Ephesians 2:20 the writer refers to his readers as "a building which rises on the foundation of the apostles and prophets...." Paul had earlier written, "No one can lay a foundation other than the one that has been laid, namely Jesus Christ" (1 Cor 3:11). Some scholars see in this contrasting emphasis evidence that the author of Ephesians is looking back on the apostolic era from some distance—and certainly from a distance greater than Paul's lifetime.

Further, the writer includes himself in the company of those who formerly "lived at the level of the flesh" (Eph 2:3). It is highly improbable that Paul, the strictest of Pharisees (Phil 3:5), ever lived like a profligate pagan, "following every whim and fancy" (Eph 2:3).

Then there is the fact that the earliest manuscripts of Ephesians do not even contain the word *Ephesus*, as we find in our modern versions of Eph 1:1. Instead, these early manuscripts simply have a blank space where *Ephesus* appears in later manuscripts, suggesting strongly that Ephesians was a circular letter addressed to *several* Churches in western Asia Minor.

While Paul himself probably wrote circular letters—Romans itself may have been one—it is unlikely that he would have sent a circular letter to Ephesus. Paul knew the Ephesian Church very well. He had lived there three years and would undoubtedly have addressed his old friends by name as he did in, for example, 1 Corinthians. He hardly would have ignored or even slighted his friends by sending them a letter with a fill-in-the-blank address.

Two concluding verses of Ephesians—6:21-22—likewise suggest non-Pauline authorship. These verses are obviously a copy of Col 4:7-8; 33 out of 34 Greek words used in the latter passage are repeated identically in the verses in Ephesians. Because of evidence such as this, most scholars today question the Pauline authorship of Ephesians.

Others defend the letter's Pauline authorship. They feel the core passages of Ephesians came from Paul himself. In such passages as Eph 6:21-22 or Eph 2:20, they posit the hand of either a contemporary secretary who touched up the work after transcribing Paul's words or a later editor who rewrote the document, incorporating into the final version both Paul's original writing as well as later reflections on that writing.

Even scholars who deny Pauline authorship of Ephesians admit that the work contains authentically Pauline thought. The difference between the "pro-Pauline" and "anti-Pauline" camps lies in *how much* of Paul's actual thought is contained in Ephesians.

THE MESSAGE OF EPHESIANS

These introductory remarks aside, let us now look at Ephesians on its own merits. Whether Paul wrote only some of it (or none of it) is really unimportant. The significance of Ephesians lies in its teaching. For the sake of convenience we will refer to the author of Ephesians as Paul.

The Microcosm and the Macrocosm

Ephesians applies to the *Church* several theological insights which Colossians had applied to the *individual*. This generalization has its limitations, but it will help us nonetheless to orient our thinking from Colossians to Ephesians.

Colossians and Ephesians represent two necessary dimensions of the concept of identification with Christ. We could label one dimension the *microcosmic* (the share of Christ's divinity to which each individual Christian is called) and the other the *macrocosmic* (the share of Christ's divinity in which humanity as a whole and all the rest of creation participates). Each dimension is an essential aspect of the same reality: the indwelling Christ in whom, through whom and for whom all creation exists.

Colossians and Ephesians thus demonstrate that Christian spirituality is a holistic spirituality—one which honors the dignity of both individual and community, giving witness to the God-likeness of *each* human being and *all* human beings. A Christian, then, cannot assert individual love for God without asserting at the same time love for all the rest of God's creation. That is because the God who is known within the individual Christian's heart is the same God who inhabits the heart of all humanity, and indeed the heart of the entire universe (Eph 1:23).

Ephesians affirms that Christians ultimately grow into identification with Christ as a community. Paul tells his individual readers, "You form a building...with Christ Jesus himself as the capstone. Through him the whole structure is fitted together and takes shape as a holy temple in the Lord." To emphasize the ongoing growth process which the entire body experiences, Paul adds, "...in him you are being built into this temple, to become a dwelling place for God in the Spirit" (Eph 2:20-22).

How the Church Identifies With Christ

In earlier works Paul treats the concept of the individual Christian's call to live a new state of consciousness. In Ephesians, he discusses the Church as a body called to live a new state of consciousness.

In this state of full development, the Church will in actuality be a new level of creation, something of a higher nature than the individual Christian and the human species itself. Paul calls this new order of creation "that perfect man who is Christ come to full stature" (Eph 4:13).

The starting point for the evolution of the Church into the "perfect man" is the transformation in consciousness of each individual believer—an idea developed by Paul in his famous prayer for his readers. It is in this prayer that we find the highest expression of Paul's theology of the Christian's identification with Christ, as well as the epitome and culmination of Paul's thought in the third stage of New Testament development:

> This, then, is what I pray, kneeling before the Father, from whom every family, whether spiritual or natural, takes its name: Out of his infinite glory, may he give you the power through his Spirit for your hidden self to grow strong, so that Christ may live in your hearts through faith, and then, planted in love and built on love, you will with all the saints have strength to grasp the breadth and the length, the height and the depth; until, knowing the love of Christ, which is beyond all knowledge, you are filled with the utter fullness of God.
> (Eph 3:14-19, JB)

Paul prays that God strengthen his readers "through his Spirit." Just as he has emphasized all along in his writings, Paul continues to stress that Christian life is not primarily a matter of will power and effort. Rather, it is a life surrendered to a higher power; it is a relationship in which human weakness is lost in God's infinite strength, conferred on the Christian through the Holy Spirit. The Holy Spirit is "the pledge of our inheritance, the first payment against the full redemption of a people God has made his own, to praise his glory" (Eph 1:14).

Thus the life in the Spirit is an evolving life; it is a life begun in God's power and brought to *full* redemption gradually. This full redemption—to return to Paul's prayer—involves the "hidden self," that is, the divine life implanted in each of us in seed form by God through the Holy Spirit. The "hidden self" is the real self, the self that God sees developing within each Christian, while the external self—the "old self which deteriorates through illusion and desire" (Eph 4:22)—dies more and more each day.

Paul prays that this hidden self will grow strong, that the seed of the Holy Spirit's indwelling will germinate, take root and flower into a life in which the Christian has attained "the utter fullness of God" (Eph 3:19). In this condition the Christian will be living the divine life which God has planned for his creation; he or she will be fully identified with Christ, living a life of Christ-consciousness.

Colossians and Ephesians present, as Paul sees it, the third stage of the love relationship which Christians enjoy with their beloved. Let us turn now to another—and very different—third-stage work.

CHAPTER EIGHT

MEDIATOR
OF A NEW COVENANT

Hebrews

T he writings we have considered thus far have been grounded principally in the Semitic thought of Jewish Palestine. The Letter to the Hebrews (Heb), while obviously written by a Jew, was written by a Jew as familiar with Greek thought as with Semitic thought. As a result, most scholars feel that the author was a man educated in an environment such as Alexandria, Egypt, where a large Jewish community existed and where Greek philosophy was particularly well-known.

Because of his reliance on Greek philosophy, the author has much in common with the author of the Johannine works which we will consider in the next chapter. Hebrews therefore serves as a good transition from Paul's theology to John's theology.

If one were to summarize the variety of scholarly guesses about the composition of Hebrews, one could say that the author—if not actually Paul's contemporary Apollos (Acts 18:24-28; 1 Cor 1:12)—was someone similar to Apollos in background and stature. Further, the writer probably wrote in Rome. He and his disciples most likely proclaimed Hebrews as a sermon, first of all to Roman Christians and then to Christians elsewhere. The author's intended audience comprised both Jewish and Gentile Christians, and his purpose was to keep those Christians from losing their faith.

The author was a man well trained both in rabbinical argumentation and Greek philosophy; he masterfully weaves each of these elements into an integrated whole. Unfortunately for us, both rabbinic argumentation and Greek philosophy are largely foreign to our

20th-century way of thinking. We cannot understand Hebrews without knowing at least a little about each. So let us first acquaint ourselves with the philosophic influence reflected in Hebrews. We will take up rabbinic argumentation later in this chapter.

THE PLATONISM IN HEBREWS

True to his Hellenistic upbringing, the author of Hebrews used the Platonic idiom of his day in expressing his ideas. Platonism stemmed from the philosophy of the great Plato (c.428-347 B.C.). Plato taught that the world of the senses is based in another world which is the "real" world. Plato's real world was based on "ideas" or "forms," by which he meant spiritual realities from which material realities took their existence.

Plato said, for example, that each and every chair which we see and touch bases its existence on, or participates in, the form "chair-ness." Chair-ness is the true reality, while all the individual chairs that we see are mere shadows or copies of the underlying reality of chair-ness. Plato's philosophy exerted a major influence on an Alexandrian Jew named Philo, who lived in the early first century and who applied many of Plato's ideas to Judaism. It was no doubt Philo who in turn influenced the author of Hebrews.

The Platonic influence pervades Hebrews. The central idea of this letter is that Christians are a people in progress from a "shadow" world (earth) to the "real" world (heaven). This passage from one world to the next has been earned for them by Jesus, the mediator of a new (real) covenant which has superseded the old Mosaic (shadow) covenant.

Here are several good examples of this Platonic idiom found in Hebrews:

> They offer worship in a sanctuary which is only a *copy and shadow* of the heavenly one.... (Heb 8:5, emphasis added)

> It was necessary that the *copies* of the heavenly models be purified in this way, but the heavenly *realities* themselves called for better sacrifices. (Heb 9:23, emphasis added)

> Since the law had only a *shadow* of the good things to come, and no *real image* of them, it was never able to perfect the worshipers by the same sacrifices offered continually year after year.
> (Heb 10:1, emphasis added)

Jesus and the Angels

The author makes a great deal about Jesus' superiority to the angels, while Christians today simply take such a belief for granted. Why, one might ask, was it so important for the early Christians to understand the fact of Jesus' superiority to angels? The answer is that many Jews in the author's time believed that angels routinely entered into and controlled the affairs of human beings.

It was important for the early Christians to understand that through Christ they had control over angels, and not the other way around. Otherwise, Christians could not truly live in a state of freedom. This point is stressed by Paul in Colossians (e.g., 2:8; 2:20-21) and may explain why the author of Hebrews uses language similar to that used in Colossians. (Compare "...all were created through him..." of Col 1:16 with "...through whom he first created the universe..." of Heb 1:2.)

Jesus, the High Priest

The author of Hebrews is preoccupied with Jesus as a great high priest and mediator of a new covenant. This theme comes to the fore in Heb 4:14—10:31. After reading this section we may be tempted to ask, "What is the significance of this?"

Christians today speak of Jesus more in terms of "savior," "Lord" or "redeemer"—titles from other New Testament books already considered—rather than in terms of "mediator of the new covenant," or "the great high priest." Yet much of our understanding of the mechanics of salvation comes from Hebrews. Hebrew's theology has made its way into the liturgy and catechesis on which many Christians were raised. For example, the Roman Catholic liturgy contains the words:

> Almighty God,
> we pray that your angel may take this sacrifice
> to your altar in heaven.
> Then, as we receive from this altar
> the sacred body and blood of your Son,
> let us be filled with every grace and blessing.
>
> (The Roman Canon, Eucharistic Prayer #1)

'Kairos,' Not 'Chronos'

One further unique characteristic of Hebrews is its understanding of time. The author of Hebrews wrote from the perspective of *kairos*

93

("vertical" time, the time of the eternal present as perceived by God) rather than *chronos* ("horizontal" or chronological time).* Unless we enter into that same perspective, we cannot understand Hebrews.

Consider this statement, for example: "But *now* he has appeared *at the end of the ages* to take away sins *once for all* by his sacrifice" (9:26b, emphases added).

The author says that Christ *has* appeared at the end of the ages—a future time. To us, accustomed to *chronos*, such a statement appears contradictory; but to someone raised in the ancient Near East—such as the author of Hebrews—the verse is not confusing at all. It expresses the intuition held by people of the author's day that for God all time is present time (*kairos*) and that by attuning oneself to God's perspective one enters into the eternal present.

The author of Hebrews constantly drives home the concept of the eternal present. In applying the Old Testament passage, "Oh, that today you would hear his voice: 'Harden not your hearts...'" (Psalm 95:7b-8), the author says, "Encourage one another daily while it is still 'today'..." (Heb 3:13)—that is, while you can still appropriate to yourselves the timeless effects of Christ's sacrifice. The author emphasizes this point again when he says, "God's word is living and effective..." (4:12), meaning his word is not something spoken "back then," but something that is eternally spoken in the present.

As heaven is the reality of which earth is only a shadow, so too *kairos* (eternal time) is the reality of which *chronos* (day-to-day time) is only a shadow. The author constantly directs his audience's attention from earth to heaven, and from day-to-day time to the eternal present.

These two conceptions of time are symbolized for the author in the old sanctuary of the Jewish Temple and the new heavenly sanctuary. The first "is a symbol of the present time" (9:9); the second is a symbol of "the time of the new order" (9:10). It is from the perspective of this "time of the new order" that Hebrews is written, and it must be read from this perspective in order to be fully understood.

HEBREWS AS A THIRD-STAGE WORK

As we might expect, Hebrews takes an approach to the Christian's identification with Christ different from that of Colossians and Ephesians.

Hebrews is not concerned with the inner transformation from

---

*A fuller discussion of these Greek words for time can be found in *The People of the Book*, p. 94.

self to Christ. Neither does it emphasize the Holy Spirit's role in bringing the Christian to a new level of consciousness—Christ-consciousness.

Hebrews sees the Christian's identification with Christ arising out of Christ's role as "mediator" (9:15) between humanity and God. "Mediator" here simply means that Christ is the one who empowers humanity to draw close to God, to become *identified* with God. Christ unites every Christian with the Father as Christ himself is united with the Father.

Prior to Christ's sacrifice such an identification had been impossible. But when Christ "appear[s] before God now on our behalf" (9:24), it is possible for humanity to claim its divine inheritance, its life in union with God in heaven.

The concept of identification in Hebrews thus takes on a different cast than that in Colossians and Ephesians. In Hebrews identification with Christ is less an earthly experience (as expressed by Paul in Gal 2:20, for example) than a heavenly reality which awaits the Christian after death.

There is in Hebrews no thought similar to Col 1:24—no suffering "lacking" which anyone can "fill up." According to the author of Hebrews, the Christian does not really advance the fulfillment of redemption; the Christian instead perseveres in awaiting that fulfillment at the end of time. For "In subjecting all things to [Christ] God left nothing unsubjected" (2:8).

The only thing left undone in salvation history, says the author of Hebrews, is fidelity to God's Word as manifested by a life of hope and perseverance. During their time of earthly existence Christians may not see all things subjected to Christ, but they are to live *as if* they see them anyway. That is why one aspect of the author's definition of faith is "conviction about things we do not *see*" (Heb 11:1, emphasis added).

All of this, of course, is in keeping with the author's Platonic perspective: It is heavenly realities which matter rather than earthly shadows. This perspective of Hebrews deserves our respect—even if it does appear at times somewhat ethereal. Hebrews reminds us that the fulfillment of our love relationship with Christ will not be experienced in this life. Only in heaven will we fully appreciate that relationship.

Paul, of course, does not disagree with this perspective. Paul's theology and that of Hebrews differ not on the fulfillment which awaits us in heaven, but on the approach to the Christian's identification with Christ. Paul believes the Christian's interior transformation begins on earth. The author of Hebrews believes in the full experience of union with Christ "reserved" for every Christian in heaven, an experience which we move toward through our daily fidelity to God's Word.

THE STRUCTURE OF HEBREWS

Hebrews is divided into three sections, corresponding to three different themes and three different understandings of the role which Christ plays in salvation history. We can summarize these divisions by means of the following chart:

Section and Theme	Christ's Role
1) Heb 1:1—4:13 God's revelation, his "Word," is spoken in his Son. This Word is superior to all previous revelations, whether delivered through angels or through holy men such as Moses.	The perfect means of communication between God and humanity
2) Heb 4:14—10:31 Christ is the new and eternal high priest whose perfect mediation establishes a new and eternal covenant between humanity and God.	The eternal high priest ever interceding before the Father on humanity's behalf
3) Heb 10:32—13:25 (Heb 12:29—13:25 is practical advice supporting the theme of the third section.) Fidelity to God's Word and hope in his promise bring Christians through the shadow reality of earth (where God's promises remain "unseen") to the true reality of heaven.	The model and examplar of Christian fidelity

1) Christ, 'Word' of the Father (1:1—4:13)

Before the incarnation of God's preexistent Son, God spoke to Israel in "fragmentary and varied ways" (1:1). Now, with the inauguration of the "final age" (1:2), God speaks to humanity perfectly and completely through the person of his Son. Since the Son is "the exact representation of the Father's being" (Heb 1:3), the Son is the perfect revelation, the perfect "Word" of the Father.

2) Christ, New High Priest (4:14—10:31)

This section is essentially a rabbinical argument to establish the author's conclusion that Christ is a new high priest eternally interceding for humanity before the heavenly throne of the Father. As we have seen, this is how the author of Hebrews sees the process of identification with Christ taking place.

Christians with no training or background in ancient rabbinical argumentation (most of us) could read this section of Hebrews and feel completely lost in a morass of esoteric and arcane scriptural references used to advance a proposition of dubious significance. The following simple outline of the steps of the author's argumentation might help in understanding this section of Hebrews.

First Step (4:14—6:20). Every high priest, the author says, shares in the human weakness of "erring sinners" (5:2), and thus is able to empathize with those for whom he makes sin offerings. Jesus, as the *ideal* high priest, likewise shared in humanity's weakness while he was on earth. "Son though he was, he learned obedience from what he suffered..." (5:8).

Second Step (7:1—8:6). To our minds this step is probably the most esoteric aspect of the author's argument. He bases this part of his argument on the shadowy figure of Melchizedek whose name appears only twice in all of Scripture (Gn 14:18-28 and Ps 110).

The author shows that Jesus is a high priest of the order of Melchizedek rather than of the order of Aaron. Thus, Jesus' priesthood is of a higher nature than "the levitical priesthood (on the basis of which the people received the law)..." (Heb 7:11). So, when God brought the ancient Levitical priesthood to perfection, he did so not in the person of a descendant of Aaron, but in the person of a "descendant" of Melchizedek.

Jesus is Melchizedek's descendant in the sense that he consecrates God's people in "perfection" (7:11), as typified by the superiority of Melchizedek's work of sanctification over that of the Levitical priesthood. (The author's logic here is not airtight, but that is not important. What matters is the ultimate point he is trying to make.)

Third Step (8:7—9:28). Not only has the old priesthood been superseded, but the old covenant between God and humanity has likewise been superseded. In the new covenant, as foretold by the prophet Jeremiah, God places his Law in the minds of his people and writes it upon their hearts (Heb 8:10; Jer 31:33).

Fourth Step: (10:1-31). Having perfected the former priesthood, and having established the New Covenant, Christ the mediator has made it possible for humanity "to draw near [to God] in utter sincerity and absolute confidence..." (10:22).

3) Jesus, Model of Christian Faith (10:32—13:25)

The author of Hebrews has no need to discuss such topics as faith-versus-works. He presumes that his audience has already exercised faith in the sense Paul uses it—that is, acceptance with one's entire being of Jesus as Lord of one's life. In other words, the author of Hebrews presumes that his readers have already reached the stage of intimacy with Christ.

For the author of Hebrews such second-stage doctrines as justification by faith represent "initial teaching" (6:1-3). He urges his readers to "advance" to the next stage. For him, Christian faith is the central virtue of this next stage of maturity.

Faith, he says, is "confident assurance [in Greek, *hypostasis*] concerning what we hope for, and conviction [*elegchos*] about things we do not see" (11:1). The author's use of *hypostasis* and *elegchos* has stimulated much scholarly discussion about the meaning of faith in Hebrews.

The *New American Bible* translation of *hypostasis* and *elegchos* as "assurance" and "conviction" suggests that faith is more of a subjective *attitude* on the part of the believer. It is thus very similar to hope, or to our concept of fidelity.

Other versions translate *hypostasis* and *elegchos* as "reality" (or substance) and "evidence." Heb 11:1 would then read, "Faith is the reality (or substance) of things hoped for, the evidence of things not seen." This gives the understanding of faith in Hebrews a more objective cast, suggesting that faith is an intuition which enables the Christian to accept God's truths.

It seems clear from reading the author's account of faith-in-action throughout Hebrews 11 that he is leaning more in the direction of the *subjective* interpretation of faith. For the author faith is not so much the acceptance of God's truths as it is the perseverance in one's acceptance previously made. Only 11:3 and 11:6b tend to oppose this conclusion. Every other verse of Heb 11 speaks of faith in the sense of a disposition or a mental attitude exercised by the believer.*

The model of this Christian faith is Jesus, who inspires and perfects our faith (12:2). To emphasize that Jesus' faith was rooted in his fidelity to the Father's will, the author uses such language as "Do not grow despondent or abandon the struggle" (12:3b); "Endure your trials as the discipline of God..." (12:7); "See to it that no man falls away from the grace of God" (12:15a).

The author of Hebrews, then, calls Christians to a final heavenly identification with Christ through a life of fidelity to God's promises. He challenges his readers to pattern their fidelity on that of Christ, the

---

*The Synoptic authors refer several times to faith in the sense of mental disposition or attitude. For example, see Mt 17:20.

model of fidelity. To emphasize this point the author closes by summarizing his message: "Jesus Christ is the same yesterday, today, and forever" (13:8).

CHAPTER NINE

'THE FATHER AND I ARE ONE'

**John's Gospel,
1, 2 and 3 John**

How does one introduce the most majestic and moving piece of spiritual literature the world has ever known? Outstripping the *Bhagavad Gita* and the *Upanishads* in its vision of the God-man, more inspiring than the *Tao Te Ching* in its depth of expression, imbued with a spirit of hope and joy which fulfills the teachings of the compassionate Buddha, the Gospel of John (Jn) is truly a spiritual masterpiece. Certainly it is the capstone of the New Testament.

In John we find the theme of the Christian's identification with Christ—the theme of the third stage of New Testament development—most beautifully and fully presented among all the works of the New Testament. John reads as if written from within Jesus' own consciousness.

John was known as the "beloved disciple," a title which perhaps indicates Jesus' own recognition of John's deep awareness of the Lord's innermost vision of life. John tells us how one becomes identified with Christ and the effects of that identification. Exceeding even Paul's achievement in developing this theme, John masterfully urges his readers on to ever deeper insights into the theme of "Christ in you" by developing more fully the role of the Father and the Spirit in the eternal union to which the believer is called.

By the conclusion of John's Gospel the Christian's participation in the life of the Trinity (not a term John used) is elaborated upon in language which would require several books to explore fully. We will make only the barest beginning here.

THE QUESTION OF AUTHORSHIP

The Church of the late second and early third centuries unequivocally verified the Fourth Gospel as being the work of John the Apostle, son of Zebedee and brother of James (Mk 1:19). One of these Church fathers—Irenaeus of Lyons—said that John "published" the Gospel rather than that he "wrote" it. Eventually such statements as this, along with the internal evidence of the Gospel itself, led later scholars to inquire more deeply into its origins.

Many scholars came to believe that it would have been impossible for an unschooled fisherman from Galilee with little if any formal theological training to write the finely polished Greek verses and profound theology which we find here. They theorized that the apostle John must have taught other writers the basic facts of Jesus' life and that these authors—writing after John's death—wove their own theology in and around the facts John had given them. Since some scholars saw this theology as similar in certain respects to second-century gnosticism, they concluded that John was written during the second century, perhaps as late as 150 A.D., in response to Gnostic attacks on Christianity.

This view has been largely set aside today. More advanced studies in the Judaism of the first century and the discovery of the Dead Sea Scrolls have caused Scripture scholars to push John's date of origin back into the first century. Some would place its writing in the late 80's, while most conclude that the mid-90's would be a more probable time frame for its composition.

Scholars have also found that first-century Judaism itself contained many of the Gnostic elements which they earlier thought had belonged to the second century. Thus, the second-century Gnostic teachings which were formerly seen as giving rise to John are now seen as actually borrowing from (and perverting) the teaching of John.

Further, Jewish fishermen in Palestine were not necessarily unlettered men. In Mk 1:20 we learn that John's father was wealthy enough to have employed "hired men." John, son of Zebedee, perhaps got the best education available in his day. For all we know he may have studied Greek from professional tutors, or even have gone to Antioch or some other major center of learning to study Greek language and philosophy.

The author of John certainly must have had some schooling in Hellenistic philosophy. Like the author of Hebrews, John's author contrasts earthly realities and heavenly realities, seeing the latter as "real" (e.g., 6:32). He uses Greek philosophical concepts like "truth" (14:6) to express his thought, and he postulates Hellenistic moral dualisms such as dark and light, death and life, spirit and flesh.

So it appears likely that the apostle John could have been responsible not only for the "facts" of the Gospel (e.g., 5:2a, 19:13), but also for the theology. John, like Jesus himself, was evidently a master of discourse, and he associated with disciples with whom he often engaged in discourse. John taught his disciples not only the details of Jesus' life; he also taught them his evaluation and conclusions concerning the *significance* of Jesus' life. This latter aspect of his teaching would, of course, have been John's theology.

There must have been several bright students among John's band of disciples—students bright enough to have challenged him to express his thought more fully or to elucidate a certain teaching more clearly.

These students probably had a more formal education in Hellenistic philosophy than John did, and thus they were undoubtedly a great help to him as he finalized his conclusions. John would have picked these students to help him edit the final version of his Gospel.

Perhaps he asked some of them to write first drafts of certain sections, or perhaps *he* wrote the first draft (or dictated it) and *they* wrote the final version. We simply don't know how the final edition came into being. John may have been alive when the Gospel was finished, but probably he was not. Nonetheless, one thing has become clearer with recent scholarship: The early Church's attribution of the Fourth Gospel to John cannot be far from the actual fact. For that reason, in the pages ahead we will refer to the author of the Fourth Gospel as John.

JOHN'S ABSTRACT LANGUAGE

Why did John use abstract, philosophical concepts in expressing himself? First of all, we must understand his Hellenistic background. Tradition has it that John lived either in Ephesus or Antioch when he wrote his Gospel, having moved to one of these cities after Jerusalem was destroyed by the Romans in 70 A.D. Since many citizens of both Ephesus and Antioch were steeped in Greek thought, it made more sense for John to express himself in Hellenistic thought patterns than in the Semitic idiom used by the earlier Gospel writers.

Further, John undoubtedly knew of the Synoptic Gospels. He presupposes many of their details in his writing. In 6:67, for example, he presumes his readers know who "the Twelve" are; he doesn't stop to identify them by name. John, therefore, doesn't replow old ground. He is interested in moving ahead to teach the deeper significance of Jesus' person and ministry rather than in simply reestablishing the fundamentals already covered by the Synoptics.

Therefore, where the Synoptics deal more in first principles, John deals more in the abstractions underlying those first principles. And since Hebrew and Aramaic thought patterns were inadequate to express these abstractions, John expresses himself in Greek thought.

Some scholars have seen in John's more theological (or more "spiritual") thought patterns, the absence of historical authenticity. They see John "off in space," as it were, writing grandiose theology which is not the least bit localized in history.

This viewpoint has likewise begun to be discredited in more recent times. For, despite its theological milieu, John is still very much rooted in history. The author is undoubtedly an eyewitness of what he observes. (This comes through even if the statement in Jn 19:35 is disbelieved.) Many details in John are even more precise than details appearing in the more "historical" Gospels such as Mark.

For example, it is John who specifically identifies such places as "Bethesda" (5:2a), the "Kidron Valley" (18:1) and "Gabbatha" (19:13), even though these sites are not at all necessary to one's understanding of the narrative. John confidently holds to his own time for the crucifixion (19:14) even though this contradicts the time which Mark remembers (Mk 15:25). It is obvious throughout his Gospel, then, that John is writing his own record of the facts.

JESUS' DISCOURSES

Nonetheless, we must still face the problem of the historicity of Jesus' discourses in John. Did Jesus—the plainspeaking carpenter of the Synoptics—really go around calling himself "the bread of life" (6:35), "the resurrection and the life" (11:25), "the way, the truth, and the life" (14:6)? Could the simple folk of Galilee and Judea have had any idea of what he was saying to them? Why is there not a single example in the Synoptics of Jesus' use of such arcane and mystical language?

The answer is that Jesus undoubtedly never used such language openly. If he used it at all it would have been with a select group of disciples, perhaps only with the Twelve or only with Peter, James and John. From the Synoptics we know that during Jesus' lifetime his disciples often could not understand what he said about himself even when he spoke plainly. They would hardly have understood what he meant by calling himself "the way, the truth, and the life."

Yet the fact that Jesus *is* the way, the truth, and the life gradually becomes obvious to us as we follow the early Church's developing

104

understanding of him through Acts, the Synoptics and the Pauline writings. Thus, while John may not have preserved in his Gospel the actual words of Jesus' discourses, he nonetheless preserves for us the underlying truth of those discourses. As a result, Jesus' discourses in John are *theological* history, in the sense that they give us an accurate record of a historical event as understood in the light of later theological reflection.

It is as if someone were to write a history of a discourse given by George Washington to a troop of colonial soldiers at Valley Forge. During the discourse the author has Washington say, "I am the father of my country." No one would believe that Washington actually referred to himself by such language during the height of the Revolutionary War. Yet after the war, when Washington became our nation's first president, it certainly became accurate to say that he *was* the father of his country.

While Washington's imagined discourse would not be historically accurate, the truth of the discourse—the substance of its teaching—*is* a historical truth when seen in the light of later patriotic reflection. In the same way Jesus' discourses in John are also historically accurate when seen in the light of the Church's subsequent theological reflection, which is precisely what is recorded by John in his Gospel.

Once again we return to our initial premise that the New Testament is the Church's book—the book of the Spirit-inspired community which grew up after Jesus' ascension. John himself acknowledges in his Gospel that it was only later, after the Spirit had come, that Jesus' disciples could fully understand who Jesus was (e.g., 12:16).

Thus, when we read Jesus' discourses in John we must read them as passages representative of the first-century Church's Spirit-inspired understanding of Jesus. As John remembers it, Jesus himself had spoken on this subject when he said,

> "...the Paraclete, the Holy Spirit
> whom the Father will send in my name,
> will instruct you in everything,
> and remind you of all that I told you." (Jn 14:26)

Since John is the New Testament writing which describes most completely the Christian's call to identification with Christ, we will spend more time discussing it than we have previous New Testament works.

The Prologue (Jn 1:1-18)

Let us look briefly at the themes John develops in his Prologue, themes which he repeats throughout the body of the Gospel:

The Preexistence of Christ (1:1-2,18). In stating this theme in the prologue John describes the preexistent Christ as "the Word" or, in Greek, *logos.* By this term John means that Christ is the ultimate revelation of the Father, in much the same sense as the author of Hebrews says, "In this, the final age, [God] has spoken to us through his Son…" (Heb 1:2).

Christ's Role in Creation (1:3). Like Paul, John too informs us that "through [Christ] all things came into being, and apart from him nothing came to be" (see Col 1:16). Interestingly, John states this theme in a different way in 1:17 where he says that through Jesus "this enduring love" (which *re*-created the world) came into being.

Jesus as Gift of New Life (1:4,16). John establishes in the Prologue a theme that becomes ever more obvious as we follow his narrative throughout the Gospel—namely, that Jesus is gift and giftbearer; he is the Father's ultimate blessing bestowed on humanity. Further, in the gift that *is* Jesus we receive *from* Jesus the gift of the Father's own divine life.

The Testimony of John the Baptist (1:6-8,15). This is a theme of lesser significance in John than in the Synoptics, perhaps because John presupposes that his readers knew from the Synoptics of the baptism of Jesus (John omits the baptismal scene). Nevertheless, John does establish the importance of the precursor's role in salvation history.

The Incarnation (1:9-11,14). In 1:14 John uses the charming Semitic expression "…and pitched his tent among us" (translated in the *New American Bible* as "made his dwelling among us") to express the mystery of the Incarnation. This, of course, is the central fact upon which all the rest of John's theology is based. Without *God's union with humanity,* which was accomplished in the Incarnation, it would not be possible for humanity to hope for *its union with God,* which is the central theme of John's Gospel. Throughout the Gospel we will constantly see how John makes allusions to the Incarnation.

The body of John's Gospel is divided by most scholars into the Book of Signs and the Book of Glory, and we will follow that division here.

The Book of Signs (Jn 1:19—12:50)

This section of John is nicknamed "The Book of Signs" because we find there seven signs performed by Jesus around which are woven the major themes that John develops in the first part of his Gospel. Before beginning this section we should first discuss John's understanding of *sign*.

The word *sign* is not synonymous with "miracle." Although Jesus' miracles in John are signs, not all of his signs are miracles. For example, the foot-washing scene of Jn 13:1-17 is a sign, though not a miracle.

For John a sign is an event which is meant to convey to Jesus' audience (and thus to John's readers) a deeper understanding of God's revelation in the person of Jesus. Jesus' signs in John, then, are generally more instructive of an underlying theological truth than are the miracles Jesus works in the Synoptics.

We can see this point exemplified in Mk 5:25-34, the story of the woman with a hemorrhage who was spontaneously healed upon touching Jesus' cloak. This miracle occurred without Jesus' even intending to cure the woman. The miracle obviously had no sign value in and of itself since Jesus didn't *use* the event to teach anyone a deeper truth of revelation. Jesus simply allowed his divine power to flow from his body—privately, we could say—to heal the woman.

In the signs which Jesus performs in John, on the other hand, there is a very definite *intended* objective in Jesus' mind. Let us look briefly at the seven signs in Jn 1:19—12:50 to see what higher truth about Jesus John intends these signs to reveal.

1) Changing Water Into Wine at Cana (2:1-11). In this sign the audience is situated at a wedding feast, a symbol used by John to suggest the Old Testament theme of Yahweh as Israel's spouse. Into the midst of this environment charged with the symbolism of marriage come Mary, Jesus and Jesus' disciples.

Suddenly, Mary notices that there is something lacking for the full celebration of the marriage feast—the celebrants have run out of wine. Wine is a symbol used by John to suggest messianic fulfillment (see Is 62:9). John is suggesting here that—because the wine, a prime ingredient of the wedding celebration, is lacking—Israel is not ready for its espousal to Yahweh. Who is to make up for this deficiency in Israel's preparation to be fully espoused to its God?

Mary explains the problem to Jesus. "Woman," he replies, "how does this concern of yours involve me? My hour has not yet come" (Jn 2:4). Despite Jesus' admonition, Mary confidently expects him to do whatever is necessary to overcome the celebrants' distress, and she instructs the waiters to follow his command.

Prompted by Mary's request, the waiters take six stone jars used "for Jewish ceremonial washings" (2:6) and fill them to the brim with water. John is suggesting here that Jewish ritual (or Judaism itself) is inadequate to bring people into a state of espousal with God. The Jewish messianic expectations will remain empty—like dry stone jars—so long as they are not turned toward the only person who can bring fulfillment to them.

By his mere word, Jesus changes the stale water of Judaism into the rich wine of the new creation which is present in his person. John concludes his account of this first sign by drawing for his readers the sign's meaning: "Thus did he reveal his glory, and his disciples believed in him" (2:11b). In other words, John is saying, the purpose of this sign was for Jesus to manifest his divinity and to call his disciples to believe.

2) Healing the Royal Official's Son (4:46-54). Jesus is back in Cana—back in the environment of his initial teaching on new creation and new life. Into that environment comes a Gentile who is in the service of Herod Antipas, one of the Herodian kings despised by the Jews. The man's son is "near death" (4:47), the condition of everyone who has yet to be affected by Jesus' saving power. The man asks Jesus to "come down and restore health to his son."

Jesus doesn't say, "Sure thing, I'm on my way!" Nor does he say, "Sorry, I'm busy at the moment." Instead, he decides to challenge the royal official to grow to a new level of awareness of Jesus' identity. He gives the man a rebuff, intended to provoke him to consider what his own interior spiritual disposition is.

"You're just looking for a miracle, aren't you?" Jesus as much as asks the man (4:48). Had the man been made of lesser fiber he might have answered, "Well, I guess you're right, but how about if I give you 50 denarii to come down and heal my son anyway?"

Instead, the man realizes that with Jesus he has found someone who operates out of higher considerations than does the ordinary miracle worker. He's not sure just *who* Jesus is, but he knows he's onto someone unlike all the other wandering prophets and magicians he's heard about. "This man's different," he thinks to himself. "He doesn't really care whether I see him perform a miracle. I think he really cares about my son's recovery." So, out of love for his son, he refuses to be put off.

"Sir," he says aloud, "come down before my child dies" (4:49). When Jesus tells him to go home, "your son will live" (4:50), he is satisfied. The man has come to a deeper awareness of Jesus' identity. All he needs is Jesus' "word" that the boy will live. The man has grown beyond his earlier need to have Jesus appear in person. Inspired by the eventual cure, the man and his entire household put their faith in Jesus (4:53b).

In this second sign John has given an example-in-action of the principle Jesus established earlier in the Nicodemus discourse (3:1-21): "...that all who believe may have eternal life in him." John shows Jesus to be the divine life-giver, the bearer of the gift of God's own Spirit.

3) A Sabbath Healing (5:1-47). The Sabbath was one of the Jews' unalterable religious institutions. To question the Sabbath and its regulations was to question the efficacy of Judaism itself; and this, of course, is precisely what John has Jesus do in this scene, by healing a man on the Sabbath. As a result, we find for the first time in John that the Jews have become determined to kill Jesus (5:18). This theme of official Jewish animosity toward Jesus becomes more and more significant as the Gospel continues.

John makes it clear that the Jews took Jesus' explanation of his Sabbath cure as a statement by Jesus of his divinity (5:18). (Jesus told the Jews in effect, "My Father works on the Sabbath, so I do too" [see 5:17].)

Jesus then uses the occasion of the Jews' opposition to him to elaborate upon his person and his mission. He tells the Jews that their self-assured faith in Yahweh depends on faith in Jesus, because it is he who truly reveals to the Jews who Yahweh is. Faith in Yahweh under the cloak of the Jewish traditions will not lead to eternal life, Jesus is saying. Only faith in Yahweh as he is revealed by Jesus leads to eternal life.

4) Multiplication of the Loaves (6:1-15) and *5) Jesus Walks on the Water (6:16-21).* John places these two signs together for a reason; we, too, will consider them together.

Throughout Jn 6, John develops his teaching on the Sacrament of the Eucharist (from the Greek *eucharistesas*, the word he uses in 6:11 for "gave thanks"). Although he omits from his Gospel Jesus' institution of the Eucharist, he still wants to suggest the connection between the multiplication of loaves and the Eucharist. He thus situates the multiplication within the context of Passover.

Notice that in Jn 6:11 Jesus himself, rather than the apostles (as in the Synoptics), distributes the bread. This is a means John uses to associate the multiplication scene with the Last Supper, where Jesus likewise distributes the bread to his apostles.

John's fifth sign follows closely upon the completion of the fourth. We notice that the fourth sign was performed before a "vast crowd" (6:2), while the fifth is performed only before Jesus' disciples (6:16)—which probably means just the Twelve, since not very many disciples would have fit within the boat. John has basically the same details in his account of the fifth sign as do the Synoptic authors in their recounting of the same event (Mt 14:22-33; Mk 6:45-52).

"The crowd" (6:22), of course, had not witnessed the fifth sign and were perplexed as to how Jesus crossed the lake to Capernaum. They ask, "When did you come here?" (6:25). John's use of irony is displayed in the answer. For the crowd means, "When did you come to Capernaum?" But Jesus' answer involves his "coming" from the Father (6:26).

Jesus then draws his listeners into a deeper level of discussion by telling them that they have sought him out simply because "you have eaten your fill of the loaves" (6:26)—that is, because they have witnessed a miracle. Yet they are missing the *sign* value of the miracle: "You are not looking for me because you have seen signs."

The Jews do not realize that the multiplication of loaves really has a deeper significance—it points to Jesus as the Son of God who feeds the Father's people with the "food that remains unto life eternal" (6:27). Jesus himself is the "bread of life" (6:48).

6) Cure of the Man Born Blind (9:1-41). This sign is a study in contrasts between the evolving spiritual consciousness of the cured blind man, on the one hand, and the Jewish elders' willed disbelief, on the other. Notice the former blind man's initial response to the question about who cured him. "That man they call Jesus" (9:11), he says, is the one. The man's words summarize the testimony of everyone who is stirred by God's revelation of Jesus Christ.

The man knows that there is something to this Jesus, but he does not understand exactly what. He can only think of the fact that "they" have been talking about him. "Jesus is somebody special; because of him something unique has happened in my life" might be a paraphrase of the healed man's first-stage response to God's action in his life.

Then, upon deeper reflection and discussion with others, the man's intellect catches up to his emotions. He is able to make a conclusion that confirms his first somewhat amorphous emotional reaction. He is able to move toward greater intimacy with Jesus. "He is a prophet," the man now replies (9:17). The man realizes that he could only have been healed by Yahweh's power channeled through a special man of God, and for a Jew the word which best describes such a person is *prophet*.

Yet the former blind man will surpass even this level of intuition into the person of Jesus. As he is pressed by the Jewish authorities to deny the reality of his cure (9:24-34), his conviction that divine power is at work in Jesus becomes all the firmer. When Jesus comes to him again (9:35), everything falls into place.

The man is now ready to be led by Jesus to a still deeper level of understanding. When Jesus at last reveals that he is the "Son of Man" (9:35,37), the Father's revelation of Jesus' identity comes spontaneously to the man's lips. "I do believe, *Lord*," he says (9:38, emphasis added). The man affirms the truth which has been gradually taking shape within his heart: Jesus is Lord—the "I AM" who he has already proclaimed himself to be to the Jews.

7) Jesus Raises Lazarus From the Dead—The Coming of Jesus' 'Hour' (Jn 11—12). This final and most powerful demonstration by Jesus that he is God's life-giver is the last straw for the authorities. If they do not move quickly, "the whole world will believe in him" (11:48)—that is, in *him* rather than in the religious institutions which are their source of wealth and power.

John uses this sign as a transition from the first half of his Gospel to the second half. This sign shows "God's glory, that through it the Son of God may be glorified" (11:4)—that the presence of the Father in Jesus may be made fully manifest. The events of the Book of Signs have been leading steadily toward Jesus' glorification, which is the subject of Jn 13—20, the Book of Glory.

Lazarus' death is actually the death to self which all Christians must undergo before they can be made into a new creation by Christ, before they can become fully identified with him. John's seventh sign teaches us that the Christian's false self must die before resurrected life, the true self of God's Spirit, can shine forth. John, of course, realizes that the *full* power of the resurrected life comes only in heaven. Yet at the same time he urges the believer to incorporate into his or her earthly existence Jesus' resurrected life, by dying a little each day to the false self and maturing to new life in Christ (see Jn 12:35).

The Book of Glory (Jn 13—20)

We saw in the Book of Signs how Jesus challenges his listeners to grow from the limited perspective of self to the unbounded perspective of God as revealed in Jesus. In those chapters John shows how Jesus is God's instrument for transforming creation from darkness to light, from ignorance to knowledge, from sin to freedom and from death to life.

With the beginning of the Book of Glory Jesus is on the threshold of his triumph. Before he ascends to glory he must form the Church which is to be the focal point of his continuing presence among humanity. Just as God's people were formed initially through Moses' promulgation of the Ten Commandments, so they must now be re-formed by Jesus' proclamation of the new and perfect commandment:

"Love one another.
Such as my love has been for you,
so must your love be for each other." (Jn 13:34)

Can human beings really love one another with Jesus' own love—a love that is infinite, unconditional, never-changing? For this to be possible we must first be transformed from self-consciousness to Christ-consciousness—we must become identified with Christ. We must reach the third stage of our love relationship with Jesus.

How does one reach this third stage? Jesus' words in Jn 14—17 are intended to show how.

Jesus tells his disciples that he is leaving but will come back to take them with him, "that where I am you also may be" (14:3). And just where *is* Jesus? Earlier he had said, "The Father and I are one" (10:30). Where Jesus *is*, then, is in union with the Father, and he wants his disciples to be there with him.

How will they accomplish this? The Father himself, upon Jesus' departure from the earth, will send "another Paraclete—to be with you always: the Spirit of truth" (14:16-17a). It is the Spirit, then, who will bring the believer to union with the Father. For when the Holy Spirit comes, Jesus says,

"...you will know
that I am in my Father,
and you in me, and I in you." (Jn 14:20)

This amazing revelation—that God calls humanity to a life of union with the Father through identification with Christ—involves a contingency. As 2,000 years of Christianity have shown, humanity is not instantaneously transformed from self-consciousness to Christ-consciousness simply by the fact that the Father sends the Spirit into the world. Christ-consciousness requires a response from humanity. And Jesus spells out the terms of this response: "Live on in me, as I do in you" (Jn 15:4).

How do we "live on in" Jesus now that he is gone? John's answer involves several levels of experience.

First Response: The Sacraments. First of all, John presupposes a sacramental cohabitation with Jesus. John alludes to this in 15:1-8. Jesus is the vine which produces the wine of Eucharist. His Church constitutes the "branches" which live in Jesus the vine.

"He who lives in me and I in him,
will produce abundantly,
for apart from me you can do nothing." (Jn 15:5)

This discourse hearkens back to the bread-of-life discourse, where Jesus says,

"If you do not eat the flesh of the Son of Man
and drink his blood,
you have no life in you." (Jn 6:53)

Second Response: Prayer. In addition to sacramental identification with Christ, John intends another level of identification—what we could call the "psychological level." Like Paul, John sees Christians as having "the mind of Christ" (see 1 Cor 2:16b). Attaining this psychological union requires attuning one's mind to the mind of Christ. Although John does not dwell on how to attain this psychological union, he clearly sees this as an important aspect of Jesus' words, "Live on in me, as I do in you" (15:4).

For John the environment which produces this psychological identification with Christ is the Church. And so, in order to appreciate fully John's teaching on this subject, we should turn to the experience of the Church as it has come to understand Jesus' words.

To do this would be beyond the scope of a book on the New Testament. But we can mention briefly that it is in the great contemplative prayer traditions of Christianity that the underlying reality of John's teaching on the psychological union of the believer and God are best elaborated. The teachings of the early desert fathers and of Benedict, Bernard, Teresa of Avila, John of the Cross and Ignatius of Loyola, for example, are a few sources to which we can turn to understand what John means by the psychological union implicit in Jn 15:1-8.

Third Response: Service. A third level of response to the call to identification with Christ is service. John makes it clear that Christian life is not simply an experience of interior consolation. Rather, Christian life involves putting into effect the love which God, through faith, puts into the Christian's heart. John, like Paul and James, believes that faith without works of loving service is useless or, better, not really faith at all.

Thus John's mysticism, like Paul's, is a this-worldly mysticism. Besides cloistered mystics there are many active mystics whose lives of service make real the Christ-consciousness which Jesus earned for humanity. In actuality it is not a question of *either* contemplation *or* action; *both* contemplation *and* action constitute the Christian's response to God's call to Christ-consciousness.

Before he goes to his glory, Jesus makes a last plea to the Father "for these you have given me" (17:9)—that is, the disciples who have followed Jesus—and "for those who will believe in me through their word" (17:20)—that is, the Church which Jesus' disciples will bring into existence with the coming of the Holy Spirit. The essence of Jesus' prayer for his Church is "that all may be one as you, Father, are in me, and I in you" (Jn 17:21).

We now see that just as Christians are to manifest in their individual lives their union with the Father, so too the Church as a whole is to manifest this state of union. Jesus prays that "*their* unity may be complete" (17:23, emphasis added), by which he means the unity of the body of believers. By living this unity Christians manifest the highest degree of their calling. And in living the deepest possible relationship with their beloved, they express the primary purpose of the third stage of New Testament development.

1 JOHN

The thought of 1 John parallels that of the Gospel of John. This fact, considered along with an ancient tradition associating this treatise with John, has led scholars to conclude that 1 John comes from the school if not the hand of the apostle.

Some scholars think that 1 John was actually written before John, almost as an abstract of the Gospel. This view is challenged by other scholars who consider 1 John to be a recapitulation of the Gospel, presented in a form that would have made it easier to circulate among Churches as a homily or catechetical text. This latter view is more consistent with 1 John's traditional status as a letter.

The themes of 1 John parallel major themes of the Gospel: light, children of God, love, faith.

The Light

The theme of light is introduced in 1 Jn 1:5—2:29. Since Jesus is "the light of the world" (Jn 8:12; 9:5), the author teaches his readers that they are to follow Jesus by walking in the light. The Christian, then, must avoid sin (1 Jn 2:1) and keep the Commandments (2:3-11). For, as in John, the author of 1 John teaches that identification with Christ is impossible unless one lives in conformity with God's Commandments:

> The way we can be sure we are in union with him
> is for the man who claims to abide in him
> to conduct himself just as he did. (1 Jn 2:5-6)

Children of God

In 1 Jn 3:1—4:6 the author elaborates upon a theme stated in the prologue to the Gospel (Jn 1:12)—the Christian's calling to be children of God:

See what love the Father has bestowed on us
in letting us be called children of God!
Yet that is what we are. (1 Jn 3:1)

Repeating the thought of 1 Jn 1:8—2:2, the author reminds his readers that as children of God they must not act sinfully. The author again exhorts God's "little children" (3:18) to keep the Commandments, the sum and essence of which is:

...we are to believe in the name of [God's] son, Jesus Christ,
and are to love one another as he commanded us. (1 Jn 3:23)

Love and Faith

The final section of 1 John repeats another important theme of the Gospel—the interplay between love and faith. As we saw in the Gospel, faith follows upon God's revelation of his Son, which is the highest expression of the Father's love for humanity:

Yes, God so loved the world
that he gave his only Son,
that whoever believes in him may not die
but may have eternal life. (Jn 3:16)

This thought is repeated in the First Letter of John:

God's love was revealed in our midst in this way:
he sent his only Son to the world
that we might have life through him. (1 Jn 4:9)

The Father's love for the world has been revealed so powerfully in the person of Jesus that the author concludes, "God *is* love" (1 Jn 4:8,16, emphasis added). And since God dwells in the believer, the believer must radiate this love to everyone else.

2 AND 3 JOHN

The Second and Third Letters of John are two miscellaneous notes associated with John's works at an early date. The "elder" of 2 and 3 John is thus supposedly John the Apostle.

The Second Letter of John is a short letter to a local Church ("a Lady" [2 Jn 1:1] is the author's symbol for Church). The letter attempts to warn the Church of the false teachings being circulated by "Antichrists" who do not accept the divinity of Jesus.

The Third Letter of John is concerned with another problem. Diotrephes, one of the Church leaders in the area, has refused to offer hospitality to traveling evangelists who have been sent out to neighboring communities at the request of the elder. The letter is addressed to Gaius, probably a Church leader in another community. The elder wants to caution Gaius's flock not to follow Diotrephes' example. Instead, they are to model their behavior on the conduct of a certain Demetrius, a Church leader who earns the elder's praise.

CHAPTER TEN

'SEE, I MAKE ALL THINGS NEW'

Revelation

In addition to the apostle John, there was another first-century John who was also a Christian writer and teacher. An early Church historian, Eusebius (c.260-340), writing in his *Ecclesiastical History*, tells us that this "other John" was a disciple of the apostle John and that he was installed as Bishop of Ephesus by the apostle John.

For centuries biblical scholars have thought of this other John referred to in the Book of Revelation (Rv) (see 1:1,4,9 and 22:8) as its author, despite an ancient tradition which associates Revelation with John the Apostle. Scholars based their conclusion on the fact that the Greek of the Book of Revelation is greatly inferior to the Greek of the Gospel of John. Further, the author of Revelation sees himself as a prophet. He never calls himself an apostle, but instead seems to segregate himself from the class of apostles to which he does refer.

Although recent scholarly opinion has found various solutions to these problems, the current scholarly consensus seems tipped in favor of the viewpoint that Revelation was written not by the apostle but by the "other John." This John was sent to the isle of Patmos by the Romans, probably because he was seen as a potential troublemaker. Patmos is in the Aegean Sea about 75 miles or so southwest of Ephesus. It was traditionally a place of banishment for political prisoners.

What kind of "trouble" did the Romans fear from John? A quick glance at the history of the period in which John wrote gives us our answer. The probable time period for the Book of Revelation is the reign of the Roman Emperor Domitian (81-96 A.D.). Domitian had

117

ordered people throughout the Empire to proclaim him "our lord and god." Christians obviously could not comply with this decree, and the Romans somehow saw in John a threat to the implementation of the decree. Hence his banishment.

Ironically, John probably did more to deter Christians from obeying the edict through his writing of Revelation than if he had simply stayed in Ephesus and preached against it. At any rate, we can now understand why a central theme of Revelation is condemnation of both Rome and worship of the Roman emperor.

The author of Revelation wrote his work out of the context of a community life shared with other Christians. While his comrades and disciples may not have actually accompanied him to Patmos, John's manuscript nonetheless would certainly have been colored by his discussions and dialogues with other Christians. Consequently, Revelation is not simply a private vision; it is a shared view of the way Christians in the late first century looked upon the Roman threat. And it is an expression of how that same community expressed its understanding of God's ultimate triumph over this threat.

HISTORICAL AND UNIVERSAL

We don't want to suggest that Revelation was written only in response to a specific historical situation with no applications for readers living in other times. Such a conclusion would be erroneous. Yet, if one had to err about the purpose of Revelation, it would be better to err in the direction of limiting the book's application to the first century than in applying the book's message solely to the 20th century. This latter application, which is commonly made today, constitutes the basic modern error in the interpretation of Revelation.

Persons who see Revelation as a book of prophecy written to advise 20th-century Christians how to prepare for the Last Day project their own viewpoint onto the author's purpose. According to these people, John used secret codes which can be understood only now as the Endtime approaches (by which conclusion they beg the question of their argument). These codes supposedly point to certain persons and places specifically seen by John long ago in his visions. The favorite speculation engaged in by proponents of this view concerns the enigmatic "666" of Rv 13:18.

People have nominated for 666 everyone from Hitler to Henry Kissinger to the various popes (who since the Reformation have been perennial favorites for the honor). It evidently has never occurred to the proponents of this view that the countless nominees for the title of

666 (or the two beasts, or Babylon the whore, or Gog and Magog, or any of the other symbols appearing in Revelation) which have been advanced by biblical literalists throughout the centuries have all proved false.

In actuality, Revelation was written not to provide secret codes that convey the specifics of the end of the world but to answer two basic questions: "How should we live in times of persecution and apostasy?" and "What is the ultimate outcome of history according to Christian teaching?" These questions were relevant for John's immediate audience (Christians living in Asia Minor in the late first century) and have continued to be relevant for his extended audience (Christians of all times and places).

Revelation does not give an exhaustive answer to these questions. It certainly does not attempt to say when the world will end or who will be in power or where the last battle will take place, etc. (If the author was attempting to pinpoint these particulars, he obviously made a mistake since he often uses such language as "very soon" to point to the last day. Two thousand years of history could hardly qualify as "very soon.")

Rather, the author is attempting (a) to describe a specific historical situation (the Roman threat to Christianity in the first century), and (b) to apply his conclusions about that situation to a universal and timeless prototype of that situation (the world's opposition to God's holiness and its refusal to accept the salvation offered to humanity through Jesus Christ).

To accomplish his purpose and to drive his message home, the author obviously had to find a way to describe both an actual historical situation and a universal situation with which all Christians of all times could identify. If he had simply said, "This book is about the Romans persecuting the Christians and how the latter found solace and hope in God's Old Testament promises and in Jesus' victory over sin and death," it might not have had an attraction for later readers. They may have viewed Revelation simply as a "period piece," with no relevance to their own lives.

Instead, by using a particular literary genre, the author was able to get his message across to both his first-century audience and all later audiences without losing any effect on either audience. If we do not understand that genre and how the author used it, we will be completely baffled by Revelation; we will either give up trying to understand it or make such mistakes as seeing 666's behind every tree on the modern world scene.

Let us look at the literary genre the author employed so we can better understand what he is trying to say to us today.*

REVELATION, APOCALYPTIC AND THE OLD TESTAMENT

The Greek word for revelation is *apocalypse*. In the last two centuries before Jesus a style of writing developed within Judaism called "apocalyptic." We could also call this "revelatory" writing in the sense that the author wrote what had been revealed to him in visions. Apocalyptic writing is not the same thing as prophetic writing, even though we do find here and there in Old Testament prophetic books passages which are apocalyptic in style (e.g., Is 24:1—27:13; Zec 1:1—6:8).

An essential difference exists between prophetic and apocalyptic writing: The prophet is principally concerned with a specific historical situation of *his own day* (condemning injustice, warning of imminent doom, calling the Jews to repentance), whereas the apocalyptic writer is describing *timeless, eternal* struggles between God and evil forces as *typified* in historical personages whose identities are hidden in symbols.

Old Testament apocalyptic writing comes into its own with the Book of Ezekiel and reaches its full flower in the Book of Daniel.†
John relied very heavily on the Old Testament in writing Revelation, and of the Old Testament books alluded to in Revelation, Ezekiel and Daniel occupy first place in importance, with Isaiah and Zechariah close behind. These are the very books which contain the greatest number of verses of apocalyptic writing.

In fact, we could really say that Revelation is an exegesis of Old Testament apocalyptic writing applied to Christian theology. One scholar has counted 278 verses out of the 404 in Revelation which are based on Old Testament passages. Yet, demonstrating his creativity, John never explicitly quotes an Old Testament verse. His usage is entirely by way of allusion and indirect references.

As an example of how John used the Old Testament, turn to Rv

---

*As our analysis will reveal, the structure, style and theme of Revelation are so unique that they prevent its inclusion in the three-stage model of New Testament development we have been using. Revelation is not so much a progression from earlier New Testament thought and theology as it is the forerunner of a whole new way of considering New Testament theology. As a result, we really can't use our "stage" model to discuss Revelation.

†Further background on Ezekiel and Daniel is found in *The People of the Book*, pp. 99-110, 129-138.

Verse From Rv 6:12-17	Old Testament Allusion
6:12—"earthquake"	Shall not the land tremble because of this, and all who dwell in it mourn? (Am 8:8a)
6:12—"sun turned black"	I clothe the heavens in mourning and make sackcloth their vesture. (Is 50:3)
6:12—"moon grew red as blood"	The sun will be turned to darkness, and the moon to blood....(Jl 3:4)
6:14—"scroll being rolled up"	The heavens shall be rolled up like a scroll....(Is 34:4)
6:14—"every mountain and island was uprooted from its base"	I looked at the mountains and they were trembling....(Jer 4:24); He rebukes the sea and leaves it dry....(Na 1:4)
6:15—"hid themselves in caves"	Get behind the rocks, hide in the dust, from the terror of the Lord....(Is 2:10)
6:16—"Fall on us!"	Then they shall cry out to the mountains, "Cover us!" and to the hills, "Fall upon us!" (Hos 10:8)

6:12-17, the scene of the "sixth seal." This passage is pregnant with Old Testament allusions, as the accompanying chart reveals.

In sprinkling Revelation with Old Testament images, John suggests to his readers that God's plan as revealed in the Old Testament is being fulfilled in the Church. Specifically, John is saying, the progression of history from the days of the Old Covenant is continuing into the days of the New Covenant. History is going somewhere: There is a past (Old Testament), present (the age of the Church) and future (the day of God's final victory over evil and God's Last Judgment). All three eras, John implies, are controlled and directed by God and pointed toward final victory for his people.

Who are God's people? Consistent with John's view of the straight line of history proceeding from the Old Testament through to Final Judgment, John sees the Church as God's people, as the "new" Israel or the fulfillment of the Israel of the past. The old Israel has completed its mission of bringing forth the Messiah; the new Israel (the Church) now undertakes its mission of bringing forth the exalted Christ of Glory, who will return as "King of kings and Lord of lords" (Rv 19:16) on the last day.

There are Christian groups today who do not accept Revelation's theology of history. They do not see the Church as the new Israel, but consider Israel as belonging to one "dispensation" (era of God's salvation) and the Church as belonging to another dispensation. They thus feel that all the promises made to Israel in the Old Testament must literally be fulfilled in today's nation of Israel. This view misses the purpose of Revelation and particularly misunderstands the Christian theology of history underlying Revelation.

A KEY TO THE SYMBOLS

John and his fellow Christians lived in a world more aware of and interested in the transcendent dimension of life than we are today. As a result, symbols were a frequent method of communication. Symbols helped to express the inexpressible; they brought the ineffable mysteries of life into focus and made them tangible.

In our day with the decline, even the eradication, of mystery and the transcendent dimension of life, symbols are not as important. We prefer to focus on what is "practical" and, consequently, tend to ignore the aspects of creation which inspire us to look beyond our senses.

Perhaps this is the reason that people in the 20th century in particular misunderstand the Book of Revelation. People whose spiritual sensitivity has atrophied are not easily able to enter into the mind-set of a first-century Jew who was well studied in the use of symbols.

To study in depth the importance and usage of religious symbolism in the society of the first century is beyond the scope of our purposes here. Instead, we will simply translate into modern terms the more frequent symbols used by John in Revelation. The following list can be referred to again and again as we read this book of the Bible.

Symbols in Revelation	Common Meaning
eyes	knowledge, wisdom
many eyes	infinite wisdom
horns (of a beast or animal)	power
long robe	priesthood
crown, diadem	kingship, royalty
whiteness	purity, victory
woman	a people, the Church
wings	mobility
trumpet	God's voice (often spoken through angels)

sword	God's spoken Word
palm leaves	victory
purple	luxury or royalty
black	death
white robes	triumph, glory
gold	royalty
lamb	Christ
Babylon	Rome
desert	spiritual purgation, persecution
four	the world, the universe in its entirety
seven	perfection, fullness
six	imperfection, inadequacy
666	absolute imperfection
12	completion
144,000 (12 x 12 x 1000)	absolute completion, fulfillment
10, 100, 1000	wholeness
3, 3½ (e.g., "a year and for two and a half years more" — Rv 12:14)	a period of calamity or persecution (not to be taken as a specific period of time)
42 months, 1260 days (3½ years)	(see above)
1/3	standard prophetic expression for "a large portion"
1600 (4 x 4 x 100) (e.g., "1600 stadia"—Rv 14:20—translated "two hundred miles" in the *New American Bible)*	the whole world

This key to the symbols in Revelation should help us adopt more of a "first-century frame of mind" as we approach this book. One more first-century predisposition will likewise be helpful: to place ourselves in the shoes of the Christians who first heard Revelation read in their assemblies. Then we will be in a good position to understand it as its author intended. For John thought of Revelation principally as *drama*, to be presented as a narration within the context of another drama—the Christian liturgy.

REVELATION AS LITURGICAL DRAMA

After a four-verse prologue Revelation begins by proclaiming that John wishes the audience "grace and peace," a familiar liturgical greeting (1:4). At the conclusion of the drama the closing words of the liturgy are pronounced: "The grace of the Lord Jesus be with you all. Amen!" (22:21). In between the opening greeting and the closing benediction, the central elements of the drama are interwoven around various liturgical hymns. For example:

All the peoples of the earth
  shall lament him bitterly.
So it is to be! Amen! (1:7b)

"Holy, holy, holy, is the Lord God Almighty,
  He who was, and who is, and who is to come!" (4:8b)

"To the One seated on the throne, and to the Lamb,
  be praise and honor, glory and might,
  forever and ever!" (5:13)

"We praise you, the Lord God Almighty,
  who is and who was.
You have assumed your great power,
  you have begun your reign." (11:17)

"Now have salvation and power come,
  the reign of our God and the authority of his Anointed One." (12:10)

"Let us rejoice and be glad,
  and give him glory!
For this is the wedding day of the Lamb;
his bride has prepared herself for the wedding.
She has been given a dress to wear
  made of finest linen, brilliant white." (19:7-8)

One can almost hear the congregation singing these verses. Undoubtedly, at least parts of Revelation were recited and sung during Christian liturgies. And this would have been consistent with John's purpose, which was to draw his readers into the drama he was presenting.

The effect on the first audiences of hearing Revelation during the liturgy must have been very powerful. Members of the audience must have thought to themselves, "Yes, that's exactly what's going on today! I see now what God is trying to accomplish in our lives." When it came time in the reading for the members of the congregation to respond in hymn, they must have found it quite easy to sing out, "Alleluia! The Lord is king, our God, the Almighty!" (19:6b).

So Revelation is not meant to be "watched" but to be participated in by all Christians as an event in the ongoing history of salvation. We are to enter into the drama through the powers of our imaginations, which the author stimulates by creatively evoking the themes of redemption through symbols.

If Revelation is drama, then *who* are its principal players, *where* does the drama unfold, and *what* happens? We can outline the drama's cast, setting and plot as follows:

Cast

Producer/Director: God the Father, "the Alpha and the Omega, the One who is and who was and who is to come, the Almighty" (Rv 1:8).

Leading Man: The Lamb—"I, Jesus,...Root and Offspring of David, the Morning Star shining bright" (22:16); "the Alpha and the Omega" (22:13). Note that the leading man shares titles with the producer/director.

Leading Lady: "Woman clothed with the sun" (12:1); Bride of Christ (19:7); the Church (21:9).

Principal Supporting Actress: Whore of Babylon—"woman seated on a scarlet beast which was covered with blasphemous names" (17:3); Rome.

Principal Supporting Actor: Devil or Satan (20:2); "huge dragon, flaming red" (12:3); the power behind the two beasts.

Additional Characters: Michael the Angel (12:7); twenty-four elders (4:4,10; 5:8; 11:16; 19:4); seven spirits before the throne—i.e., God's Spirit manifesting itself in fullness (1:4; 3:1; 4:5; 5:6); four horsemen—Oppression, War, Famine, Epidemic (6:1-8); first beast—10 horns and seven heads, the Whore of Babylon under another guise (13:1); second beast—servants of the first beast, the imperial priesthood (13:11); four "living creatures"—lion/nobility, man/wisdom, ox/strength, eagle/mobility (4:6); numerous angels.

Chorus: "One hundred and forty-four thousand from every tribe of Israel" (7:4); "huge crowd" (7:9); those who "have washed their robes and made them white in the blood of the Lamb" (7:14); the elect.

Setting

Throne Room in Heaven (4:1-11). Throne encircled by rainbow (suggesting God's mercy—Gn 9:12) and situated on crystal-clear glass floor. Twenty-four smaller thrones surrounding God's throne. Twenty-four elders clothed in white garments with gold crowns on their heads. Thunder and lightning. Seven torches burning before the throne. Four living creatures praising God day and night without pause. Abode of the Lamb.

Earth (12:4a). The location of the seven (i.e., "all") Churches (1:4—3:19). The time of the present. The Christian's day-to-day involvement in the cosmic struggle going on all around the earthly Church. Habitation of the two beasts (i.e., all earthly power opposed to God).

The Heavens. Place where the plot unfolds. The battleground for the spiritual warfare in which God ultimately defeats Satan and all the powers of evil.

Plot

Imagine you are seated in a huge amphitheater waiting for the drama to begin. A man walks onstage and says, "This is the revelation God gave to Jesus Christ, that he might show his servants what must happen very soon" (Rv 1:1a). This stirs your sense of suspense and you pay closer attention.

"I wonder whether the outcome of this drama will be good or bad," you ask yourself. The narrator gives you a clue: "Happy are you who hear this message and heed it" (based on 1:3).

"Aha! A 'message'!" you think. "I'd better pay close attention. There's going to be a moral to this story."

Message to Seven Churches. The drama begins on earth. The author wants to situate his audience firmly within the confines of the cosmic struggle about to be described. Yet he wants the audience to understand that this struggle takes place on earth also, and that it affects the Christian in his or her day-to-day life in the Church. Thus he gives an introductory view of seven Churches, by which he means the Church as a whole, intending to illustrate how the Church must attend daily to its role in the cosmic struggle.

John reads to the seven Churches advice revealed to him by God. The seven Churches are local Churches in the vicinity of John's headquarters, the Church of Ephesus. John's words of praise and admonition are to be read as general advice to the Church of his day about spiritual concerns.

Having heard the messages to their local Churches, the audience is properly prepared to enter into the ensuing conflict; it now knows that what is to follow affects its own daily existence. "Let him who has ears heed the Spirit's word to the churches" (3:22), the author says, as he now turns the audience's attention from earth to heaven.

The Seven Seals. In a scene reminiscent of Ezekiel 1 and 10, John brings the audience into God's heavenly court. The cosmic struggle which is about to be unleashed has its origin in the breaking open of a scroll sealed by "seven seals" (Rv 5:1)—that is, a scroll absolutely locked to humanity's comprehension. To center stage comes a Lamb with "seven horns and seven eyes" (5:6)—that is, Christ possessed of absolute power and knowledge. To him has been given the authority to open the scroll—to initiate the last era of history, the coming of God's final judgment and his victory for the elect.

The drama now begins in earnest. The Lamb begins to open the seven seals one by one. With the breaking of the first four seals, four horsemen ride forth distributing persecution, war, famine and sickness. This is the human condition prior to God's judgment and is meant to represent all of human history. The message is that God permits suffering until his victory can be completed; suffering is a part of God's salvific plan.

With the breaking of the fifth seal, God introduces martyrdom into human history (history seen here as *all* ages of the past, even before the time of Jesus). God's martyrs (from the Greek *martyria*, or "witness") are those who have been called in a special way—by laying down their lives—to witness to God's holiness in the face of evil. The martyrs are told to "be patient a little while longer until the quota was filled of their fellow servants and brothers to be slain, as they had been" (6:11).

With the opening of the sixth seal, we reach the last moment of earthly history. Before God comes in glory, John says, nature itself will give testimony to the evil that it has harbored all these many centuries. (Compare Mk 13:8; Mt 24:7.) The great day of God's vengeance upon this evil has now come (Rv 6:17), and thus we are ready for the opening of the seventh seal.

To set the stage for the events that follow the opening of the seventh seal, the author pauses to inject into the drama the theme of victory. All of saved humanity (the 144,000 of Rv 7:4) are brought onstage into the heavenly court. The Lamb breaks open the seventh seal and, like a lull before a storm, "there was silence in heaven for about half an hour" (8:1). Then begins the period of cataclysms attendant to the ushering in of God's final judgment.

John parallels these cataclysms to the great plagues of Exodus, once again illustrating the theme of the continuity of salvation history. Just as God punished Pharaoh for holding the Israelites in captivity, so now the new Pharaoh (the world, typified in the Roman Empire) must be punished for keeping the Church, the new Israel, imprisoned in a climate of oppression, persecution and evil.

Satan and the Church. The final act of the drama finds Satan desperately trying to destroy the Church (Rv 12). War breaks out "in heaven" (12:7) between the spiritual forces of good—championed by Michael—and the evil forces—led by Satan and the fallen angels. Michael drives Satan out of heaven and onto earth, where he attacks the "woman" (the Church).

For an indefinite period of time (12:14) the Church is preserved from harm, even though it must undergo the "desert" of persecution brought upon it by Satan's chief lieutenants on earth. These lieutenants are the two beasts: Rome (the beast with 10 horns and seven heads—13:1), and the imperial priesthood (the beast with "two horns like a ram"—13:11, which speaks "like a dragon," that is, in the name of Satan).

The two beasts represent worldly power and false religion, the two powers most opposed to God's rule on earth. The second beast "used the authority of the first beast to promote its interests by making the world and all its inhabitants worship the first beast..." (13:12). Further, the second beast performed "great prodigies" (13:13) to impress humanity with its spiritual prowess. Just so the reader understands who the symbols of the beasts represent, John pauses to give his audience a clue: The "number" of the beast stands for "a certain man"; "the man's number is six hundred sixty-six" (13:18).

The Number 666. To understand this symbol we must understand the ancients' fascination with numerology—the study of the hidden significance of numbers.

An inscription from the ruins of Pompeii records this delightful note: "I love her whose number is 545." In ancient numerology each letter of the alphabet was given a numerical equivalent, and then totalled in order to arrive at a person's "number." Precise predictions about a person's character supposedly followed from knowing his or her number.

Who does John intend by 666? In Hebrew the name for Nero Caesar (the most dreaded of Roman emperors for early Christians) was spelled NRWN QSR. Applying a numerical-alphabetical table prevalent in John's time, the letters add up to 666. This conclusion would obviously be in keeping with John's condemnation of Rome's wickedness.

Yet whoever John intends by 666, his purpose in choosing the number is clear. The opponents of God exist in a state of absolute imperfection, symbolized by 666, the number which falls short of the symbol for absolute perfection—seven and its combinations.

God's Ultimate Victory. After introducing the two beasts, John quickly leads us to the moment of their demise. Another angel comes forth and announces, "Honor God and give him glory, for his time has come to sit in judgment" (14:7). In the person of the resurrected Christ—the One like a Son of Man of Dn 7:13—judgment begins (Rv 14:14). Prolonging the suspense perhaps a bit too long, John repeats in Rv 15—16 essentially the same pre-judgment cataclysms of Rv 8—9.

(We could just as well have passed right to Rv 17 without this redundant interlude.) Finally, after telling us who the beast is (17:8—it is obviously Rome), and having the choir come back onstage to sing the final chorus of victory (18:2—19:8), the slaughter of the wicked is accomplished.

Having promised his audience victory and happiness in his opening chapters, John now delivers. The world is created anew; the Church likewise shines forth in heavenly glory. The "new Jerusalem" (21:2)—the abode of Christ victorious—replaces the old Jerusalem, the Church on earth—the abode of Christ suffering. Everything in John's heavenly city suggests fullness and completion. The walls of the city described in Rv 21:16, for example, form a perfect square "twelve thousand furlongs in length, in width, and in height" (12,000 = 1000 × 12, or perfect fulfillment).

To complete his act of re-creation, God the Father speaks for the first time in Revelation. "See, I make all things new" (21:5). History, having begun with God's creation in Genesis, now concludes with his re-creation in Revelation. Revelation is thus the Christian theology of history; it explains the purpose of existence and of time in terms of the end-point of existence and time—God's final victory for his people and his re-creation of all things.

The drama having concluded, the "narrator" returns to the stage (22:8-21). Lest anyone in the audience doubt the veracity of this amazing production, the playwright himself now appears to put his personal seal of authenticity on the script: "I myself give witness to all who hear the prophetic words of this book" (22:18). To still any remaining doubts, the Lord himself authenticates John's transcription of the revelation: "The One who gives this testimony says, 'Yes, I am coming soon!'" (22:20). The audience responds, "Amen! Come, Lord Jesus!"

CONCLUSION

After finishing Revelation, we may feel like asking, "What now?" or, "Where do we go from here?"

Where *do* we go from here? We now know how the story ends. We know that God's holiness will prevail in the end, and that those who have chosen to accept God's call to union through his Son will live in eternal happiness.

So what do we do in the meantime? Do we sit in the theater waiting for the final act in the drama, or do we enter into the drama ourselves? Are we spectators or participants? Our answer to that question says a lot about how we look upon the New Testament (and the rest of the Bible).

CHRISTIANITY: A SPECTATOR SPORT?

If we see the Bible as a book delivered by God from "up there" to us "down here," then we are apt to see God's Words in Scripture as immutably fixed and emanating from a realm we can enter only after death. By this view, our relationship with God revolves around our living *in* the book, as it were, without ever really stepping forth into the world where the book is located. The Bible becomes an end in itself, and our lives as Christians are entirely bound up with service to the Bible, rather than with service to God's people and his world.

In my Bible classes I like to stir things up by telling my students that if they hold to the fundamentalist view of the Bible, I hope they go to a heaven where the principal act of worship is performed before a hundred-foot-high monument of a book inscribed "Holy Bible." (After the laughter dies down I add, "Or perhaps you would choose a heaven where this monument is replaced by a scale model of St. Peter's Basilica." That usually quiets my Catholic audiences.) The point is that we are called to serve and love a living God—not a book (or, equally as bad, an institution).

If, on the other hand, we have entered into the perspective from which I have written this book—the story *behind* the New Testament—then we realize that God gave us his revealed Word not from "up there," but while *among us*—right where the Kingdom of heaven in seed form is located (Lk 17:21). And since God chose to reveal himself through the human authors of Scripture, as well as to come among us himself, he still lives among us now—in the Bible and in his people.

Thus, the Bible, apart from being a sacred book, is also a tool which helps us live in the real world. Scripture is not an end in itself but a means to an end—the means by which we transform ourselves from self-consciousness to Christ-consciousness, so that we may build up God's Kingdom on earth according to the mind of Christ.

A HUMAN JESUS, A HUMAN BIBLE

Unless we believe that the Bible is the work of God among us, then we will hardly be able to believe that God is *among us* still or, further, that his being among us makes any difference.

For 2,000 years Christians have been trying to take Jesus' humanity away from him and relegate him to the great beyond where, for reasons of our own inability to take God's Word seriously, we wish he would remain. By looking upon Jesus in this way we don't have to answer for ourselves embarrassing questions about why Christianity has little if any influence in the world today. If Jesus is "out there somewhere" then, of course, he is not concerned about hunger, the buildup of nuclear arms, poverty, social injustice and all the other evils confronting the world.

Just as we have done with Jesus, we likewise tend to strip the Bible of its humanity. We overlook the fact that, just as divinity and humanity are inseparably united in Jesus, so too are they inseparably united in the Bible. Because of this oversight, the Bible often becomes little more than an unapproachable talisman, transcending the real world of sin and suffering.

If, on the other hand, we believe that Jesus is among us still,

132

through the power of his Holy Spirit, in the words of Scripture and in his people, then we know that Christianity is empowered to confront and overcome the evils in the world. And the Bible becomes not simply an attractive religious object, but a flaming sword (or, to be more contemporary, a *Star Wars* light saber) which we use to build up the Kingdom of God on earth.

A People of 'the Way'

In the process of building up God's Kingdom we cannot help but grow through the stages of Christian maturity which the early evangelists presented—each in his own way—in the New Testament works we have just analyzed. We thus reproduce in our own lives the stages of New Testament development, growing from infatuation with Jesus to intimacy and eventually to identification with him. This book was written for people who see in Jesus "the way"—who, in fact, believe Jesus is *the* Way and want to become one with him.

If we do not read the New Testament in this way, it cannot be the "power of God leading everyone who believes in it to salvation" (Rom 1:16), as it was intended to be. At best, the New Testament will be for us only a curiosity piece. At worst, it will become an idol—a religious rabbit's foot which we wave and thump and holler over while the Kingdom of God shrinks ever more into insignificance in today's world.

We thus return to our starting point: The Bible is the Church's book. We read it, understand it and implement its message only in contact with the community which gave it to us and which has sustained and treasured it through the centuries. By looking at the New Testament in this way we can come to understand it on its own terms—as it was intended by those first-century seekers of truth who were willing to trade life itself for the ultimate answer to their question, "Who is Jesus of Nazareth?"

SCRIPTURE INDEX

Genesis
9:12 — 125
14:18-20 — 97

Leviticus
19:18b — 67
25 — 62
25:47-55 — 62

2 Samuel
7:13 — 12

Psalms
95 7b-8 — 94
130:7 — 62

Isaiah
2:10 — 121
24:1—27:13 — 120
34:4 — 121
50:3 — 121
53:8 — 12
61:2 — 32
62:9 — 107

Jeremiah
31:33 — 97

Ezekiel
1 — 126
10 — 126

Daniel
7:13 — 12, 128
7:14 — 12

Hosea
10:8 — 121

Joel
3:4 — 121

Amos
8:8a — 121

Nahum
1:4 — 121

Zechariah
1:1—6:8 — 120

Malachi
3:23 — 34

Matthew
1:1-17 — 30
3:1—4:11 — 24
4:12—18:35 — 24
4:18-20 — 24
5:1-12 — 31-32
5:3 — 33
5:6 — 33
5:17 — 29
8:27-30 — 25
11:28-30 — 52
14:22-33 — 110
16:13-20 — 34
16:13-16 — 25
16:17 — 35
16:18 — 29
17:20 — 98
18:1-35 — 29
19:1—20:34 — 25
19:25 — 33
19:26 — 34
21—28 — 25
23:4b — 52
24:7 — 127
24:36 — 42
28:19 — 86

Mark
1:1—8:26 — 28
1:1-13 — 24
1:14—9:50 — 24
1:19 — 102
1:20 — 102
1:24 — 28
1:44 — 28
2:10 — 28
3:12 — 28
3:21 — 74
5:25-34 — 107
5:43 — 28
6:3 — 74, 77
6:45-52 — 110
7:3-4 — 27
7:36 — 28
8:26 — 28
8:27—16:20 — 28
8:27-30 — 34
8:30 — 28
8:31 — 28
8:32 — 28
8:34-35 — 47
8:34 — 28
9:9 — 28
9:23 — 28
9:24 — 28
10:1-52 — 25
11—16 — 25
13:8 — 127
14:12 — 27
15:25 — 104
15:42 — 27

Luke
1:35 — 17, 30
2:7 — 74
3:1—4:13 — 24
3:15 — 33
3:21-22 — 30
3:23-38 — 30
4:14—9:50 — 24
5:11 — 31
6:17-26 — 32-34
6:45b — 67
6:49 — 67
7:36-50 — 31

9:18-21	25, 34	14:20	112	1:16	27, 61, 63, 132
9:23	5, 31	14:26	105		
9:43	33	15:1-8	112, 113	1:18—3:20	61
9:51—18:43	25	16:7	16	3:24	62
12:22-31	31	17:9	113	4:13b	61
12:39	42	17:20	114	5:8	67
15:1-10	31	17:21	114	5:9	62, 63
15:11-32	31	17:23	114	5:10	62, 63
17:21	132	18:1	104	6:1—8:39	64
18:9	33	19:13	103, 104	6:4-5	83
19—24	25	19:14	104	6:6	64
19:1-10	31	19:25-26	3	6:11	64
		19:35	104	6:12	64
				7:4	64
John		**Acts**		7:6	64
1:1-18	106	1	17	7:7, 8, 12	64
1:12	115	1:13	74	7:18b	64
1:19—12:50	106-111	2	17, 30	7:19	64
2:1-11	107-108	2:14-41	17	7:22	64
3:1-21	109	2:38-39	25	7:25	64
3:16	115	4	30	8:14-16	65
4:46-54	108-109	9:3-19	40	8:18	66
5:1-47	109	10	18	8:21	66
5:2a	103, 104	11:20	18	8:22	86
6:1-15	109-110	11:22	18	8:23	65
6:16-21	109-110	11:26b	18	8:26-27	66
6:22	110	12:1	74	8:31	66
6:25	110	12:12	27	9:27	63
6:26	110	12:25	27	10:9	63
6:27	110	13	18	10:10	63
6:32	102	13:44-52	18	10:13	63
6:35	104	15	75	12:1	66
6:48	110	15:37-39	27	12:2	66
6:53	113	16:9b	53	12:10b, 12, 13b,	
6:67	103	17:1-9	40, 41	14, 17a, 18;	
8:12	114	18:1, 18	40	13:1, 6, 8,	
9:1-41	110-111	18:24-28	91	13	67
9:5	114	19:23-40	53	13:9	67, 78
10:30	112	20:31	53	13:11	63
11—12	111	22:6-16	40		
11:4	111	23:16	39	**1 Corinthians**	
11:48	111	26:12-18	40	1:10-12	44
11:25	104	28:24	19	1:12	91
12:16	105	28:30	19	1:30	62
12:35	111			2:16b	113
13—20	111-114	**Romans**		3:1-2	3
13:1-17	107	1:1	60	3:11	87
13:34	112	1:2	60	5:9	43
14—17	112	1:4	61	6:12	46
14:6	102, 104	1:10-13	59	6:15	46
14:16-17a	112				

6:17	46
6:18	44
6:19-20	46
7:3	46
7:5	44, 46
7:17	46
12—14	46
12:12-26	47
12:27	47, 85
12:28-30	47
14:4	47
15:1-11	15
15:7	75
15:28	85

2 Corinthians

2:4	44
5:17	2
6:2	63
12:14	44

Galatians

1:11—2:14	15
1:12b	57
1:17-18	40
1:19	74
2:14b	57
2:16a	57
2:20	78, 95
5:1, 4	57
5:13	57
5:19-21a	58
5:22-23	58
6:1-2	58
6:15	58
8:21	58

Ephesians

1:1	87
1:14	89
1:23	88
2:3	87
2:20-22	88
2:20	87
3:14-19	89
3:19	89-90
4:13	89
4:15	86
4:22	89

| 6:21-22 | 87 |

Philippians

1:1—3:1a	53
1:13	53
1:21-26	54
2:2-4	54
2:6-11	54
2:25-28	53
3:1b—4:4, 8-9	54
3:2	54
3:4	54
3:5	87
3:9b	54
3:13a, 15a, 16	54, 55
4:4-7	53
4:7-8, 33	87
4:8	66
4:10-20	53
4:21-23	53

Colossians

1:9	86
1:15	84
1:16	83, 84, 93, 106
1:17	84
1:18	85
1:19	83
1:24	86, 95
1:28	86
2:8	93
2:9	83, 86
2:12	83
2:18	83
2:20-21	93
4:12	86

1 Thessalonians

4:15	42
4:16b-17a	42
5:13b	42
5:14	42
5:15	42
5:17	42
5:20	42

2 Thessalonians

2:3	43
2:15	43
3:10	43

1 Timothy

1:10	71
3:2-5	72
3:8	73
3:8, 10, 12	72
3:14-15	73
3:15	71, 72, 73
4:6	71
4:13	73
4:14	72
4:15-16	73
5:17, 19	72
5:17	73
6:3	71, 72

2 Timothy

| 2:22 | 73 |
| 4:3 | 71 |

Titus

1:6	72
1:7	72
1:8	73
1:9	71
2:1	71

Philemon

16	78
17	78
21	78

Hebrews

1:1—4:13	96
1:1	96
1:2	93, 96, 106
1:3	96
2:8	95
3:13	94
4:14—10:31	93, 96-97
4:14—6:20	97
5:2	97

5:8	97
6:1-3	98
7:1—8:6	97
7:11	97
8:5	92
8:7—9:28	97
8:10	97
9:9	94
9:10	94
9:15	95
9:23	92
9:24	95
9:26b	94
10:1-31	97
10:1	92
10:32—13:25	96, 97-99
11	98
11:1	95, 98
11:3	98
11:6b	98
12:2	98
12:3b	98
12:7	98
12:15a	98
12:29—13:25	96
13:8	99

James

1:1	73, 74
2:2	75
2:18b	76
2:24	76
2:14-16	75-76

1 Peter

1:13b	77
1:22	76
2:13	76
2:15b	76
5:13	27

2 Peter

1:15-17	77
2:1-18	77
3:1	77
3:8	77
3:15-16	77

1 John

1:5—2:29	114
1:8—2:2	115
2:1	114
2:3-11	114
3:1—4:6	115
3:1	115
3:18	115
3:23	115
4:8, 16	115
4:9	115

2 John

1:1	116

Jude

1:3b	77

Revelation

1:1a	126
1:1, 4, 9	117
1:3	126
1:4—3:19	125-126
1:4	123-124, 125
1:7b	124
1:8	125
3:1	125
3:22	126
4:4	125
4:5	125
4:6	125
4:8b	124
4:10	125
5:1	126
5:6	125, 126
5:8	125
5:13	124
6:1-8	125
6:11	126
6:12-17	120-121
6:17	127
7:4	125, 127
7:9	125
7:14	125
8—9	129
8:1	127
11:16	125
11:17	124

12	127
12:1	125
12:3	125
12:7	125, 127
12:10	124
12:14	123, 128
13:1	128
13:11	128
13:12	128
13:13	128
13:18	118, 128
14:7	128
14:14	128
14:20	123
15—16	129
17	129
17:3	125
17:8	129
18:2—19:8	129
19:4	125
19:6b	124
19:7	125
19:7-8	124
19:16	121
20:2	125
21:2	129
21:5	129
21:9	125
21:16	129
22:8-21	129
22:8	117
22:13	125
22:16	125
22:18	129
22:20	129
22:21	124

TOPICAL INDEX

Aaron, 97
Abraham, 30
Acts of the Apostles, 4, 8-9, 11-19, 25, 41, 74, 105
Adam, 30
Adelphos, 74-75
Alexandria, 91
Amu Darya, 49
Ananias, 40
Ancyra, 50, 57
Angels, 84-85, 93
Anointed one, 12, 18. *See also Christos*, Messiah.
Antichrist, 43
Antioch, 16, 18, 29, 57, 102-103
Apocalypse, the, 43, 120. *See also Revelation.*
Apocalyptic literature, 120
Apollos of Alexandria, 8-9, 91
Apostle(s), 18, 39, 74, 102, 109, 114, 116-117. *See also* the Twelve.
Aquinas, Thomas, 60
Asia, 49-50, 53
Asia Minor, 16, 87, 119
Athens, 41
Babylon (the whore), 119, 123, 125
Baptism of Jesus, 106
Barnabas, 18, 27
Beatitudes, the, 31-34
Benedict, 113
Bernard, 113
Beroea, 41
Bethesda, 104
Bishops, 72-73
Bithynia, 49
Body of Christ, the, 46-47, 85-86
Book of Glory, the (*John*), 106, 111-114
Book of Signs, the (*John*), 106-111
Bride of Christ, the, 125
Cana, 107-108
Capernaum, 110
Cappadocia, 49
Chloe, 43-44

Christ-consciousness. *See* Identification.
Christos, 18. *See also* Anointed one, Messiah.
Chronos, 93-94. *See also Kairos*, Time.
Cilicia, 39
Colossae, 40
Colossians, 40, 84, 88
Colossians, 5, 8-9, 79, 83-86, 90, 93, 94-95
Corinth, 40, 43-44, 46, 49-50, 57-58
Corinthians, 15, 40, 43-46
1 Corinthians, 4, 8-9, 15, 41, 43-47, 53-54, 57, 67, 83, 87
2 Corinthians, 4, 8-9, 41, 43-47, 54, 57, 67
Cornelius, 18
Crete, 72
Cross, the, 5, 28, 47
Cyprus, 18
Cyrene, 18
Damascus, 38-40, 52, 83
Daniel, 12, 120
David, 12, 60
Day of the Lord, the, 32, 43. *See also* the Endtime, the End times, the Final Coming, the Last Day, the Last Judgment, the Parousia, the Second Coming.
Deacons, 72-73
Dead Sea Scrolls, 102
Derbe, 57
Deuteronomy, 29
Devil, the (Satan), 125, 127-128
Diotrephes, 116
Domitian, 117-118
Ecclesiastical History, 117
Ekklesia, 29
Elders, 72-73
Elijah, 34

Endtime, the, 63, 118. *See also* the
Day of the Lord, the End
times, the Final Coming, the
Last Day, the Last Judgment,
the Parousia, the Second Com-
ing.
End times, the, 41-42. *See also* the
Day of the Lord, the Endtime,
the Final Coming, the Last
Day, the Last Judgment, the
Parousia, the Second Coming.
Epaphroditus, 53
Ephesians, 40, 87, 94
Ephesians, 5, 8-9, 79, 83, 85-90, 95
Ephesus, 40, 43-44, 53, 72, 87, 103,
117-118, 126
Eschatology, 41, 83
Esther, 11
Eucharist, the, 109, 112
Eusebius, 117
Exhortation, 75, 77
Exodus, 29, 127
Ezekiel, 11
Ezekiel, 120
Ezra, 11
Faith, 55-56, 75-76, 95, 97-99, 109,
113, 115
Final Coming, the, 42. *See also* the
Day of the Lord, the Endtime,
the End times, the Last Day,
the Last Judgment, the
Parousia, the Second Coming.
First stage of New Testament
development, the, 4, 15, 17,
19, 61, 79, 110. *See also*
Infatuation.
Four horsemen, the, 125, 127
Freedom, 51, 57-58, 61, 66-67, 73,
82.
Fundamentalist(s), 72, 131
Gabbatha, 104
Gaius, 116
Galatia, 40, 50-51, 56-57
Galatians, 40, 56-57
Galatians, 4, 8-9, 51-53, 55-58
Galilee, 13, 30, 61, 102, 104
Gamaliel, 39
Genesis, 129
Gentiles, 12, 16-19, 27, 30, 44,
54, 57, 59, 108

Gentile Christians, 19, 44, 59, 91
Gnosticism, 84-85, 102
Gog, 119
Greece, 30
Greek philosophy, 91, 104. *See also*
Hellenistic philosophy,
Platonism.
Hebrews, 5, 8-9, 60, 79, 91-99,
102, 106
Hellenistic philosophy, 102-103. *See
also* Greek philosophy,
Platonism.
Herod, 74
Herod Antipas, 108
Herodians, 12
Iconium, 57
Identification, 5, 8-9, 55, 78-79, 83,
86, 88-90, 94-96, 98, 101,
105, 112-114. *See also* the
Third stage of New Testament
development.
Ignatius of Loyola, 113
Incarnation, the, 106
Infatuation, 3-5, 8-9, 15, 17, 19, 31,
35, 41, 46-48, 52, 55, 58, 60-
61, 65, 67, 83, 85, 133. *See
also* the First stage of New
Testament development.
Intimacy, 4, 5, 8-9, 19, 28, 31, 35,
41-42, 47-48, 52, 55, 58, 60,
64-65, 67, 69-70, 78, 83, 86,
98, 110, 133. *See also* the
Second stage of New
Testament development.
Irenaeus of Lyons, 102
Isaiah, 11-12
Isaiah, 120
Israelites, 1, 127
James, 4, 8-9, 69, 73-77
James the Apostle (brother of John),
73-74, 102, 104
James ("the brother of the Lord"), 57,
73-75
James the Lesser, 74
Jeremiah, 11, 13, 97
Jerusalem, 11, 27, 29, 37-38, 40, 44,
57, 75, 81, 103
Jewish Christians, 28-29, 32, 44, 59,
75, 91

Johannine Epistles. *See* 1, 2
   and 3 John.
John, 6, 8-9, 13, 18, 74, 101-104,
   114, 116-117
John, 5, 8-9, 24, 79, 91, 101-114,
   117
1 John, 5, 8-9, 79, 91, 114-115
2 John, 5, 8-9, 79, 91, 116
3 John, 5, 8-9, 79, 91, 116
John the Baptist, 106
John of the Cross, 82, 113
John of Ephesus, 8-9, 117-118, 122,
   126, 128
John Mark, 27. *See also* Mark.
John, School of, 8-9, 103, 114
Joses, 74
Judaism, 1, 16, 52, 57, 92, 102, 108-
   109, 120
Judaizers, the, 52, 54-55, 57-59
Judas, 74, 77. *See also* Jude.
Jude, 77. *See also* Judas.
Jude, 4, 8-9, 69, 77-78
Judea, 104
Judith, 11
Justice, 55. *See also* Justification.
Justification, 55-58, 61, 63-66, 76,
   98. *See also* Justice.
Kairos, 93-94. *See also Chronos*,
   Time.
Kerygma, 14-15, 25-26, 30-31, 41.
   See also Proclamation.
Kidron Valley, 104
Lamb, the, 124-127
Last Day, the, 118. *See also* the Day
   of the Lord, the Endtime, the
   End times, the Final Coming,
   the Last Judgment, the
   Parousia, the Second Coming.
Last (Final) Judgment, the, 77,
   121. *See also* the Day of the
   Lord, the Endtime, the End
   times, the Final Coming, the
   Last Day, the Parousia, the
   Second Coming.
Last Supper, the, 109
Law, the, 31, 38, 39, 51-52, 54-55,
   58, 64, 74, 92, 97
Levitical priesthood, 97
Leviticus, 62
Luke, 8-9, 14-17, 30-31, 33

Luke, 4-5, 8-9, 17, 19, 24-27, 30-35,
   74. *See also* the Synoptic
   Gospels.
Lystra, 57
Maccabees, the, 11-12
Maccabeus, Judas, 12
Macedonia, 40-41, 44, 50, 53
Magog, 119
Mark, 8-9, 27. *See also* John
   Mark.
Mark, 4-5, 8-9, 19, 24-31, 34-35,
   47, 104, 107. *See also* the
   Synoptic Gospels.
Mary, 30, 74-75, 107
Matthew, 24, 29, 31
Matthew, 4, 8-9, 19, 24-27, 28-35.
   See also the Synoptic Gospels.
Matthew, School of, 8-9, 29
Melchizedek, 97
Merton, Thomas, 78
Messiah, 2, 4, 12-14, 16-19, 23,
   27-29, 32, 34-35, 40, 74, 82,
   107-108, 121. *See also*
   Anointed one, *Christos*.
Messianic secret, 28-29
Metanoia, 2
Michael the Angel, 125, 127
Miracles of Jesus
      Changing of Water Into Wine
         at Cana, the, 107
      Cure of the Man Born Blind,
         the, 110
      Healing of the Royal Official's
         Son, the, 108
      Healing of the Woman With a
         Hemorrhage, the, 107
      Multiplication of the Loaves,
         the, 109
      Raising of Lazarus From the
         Dead, the, 111
      Sabbath Healing, the, 109
      Walking on the Water, 109
Mosaic Covenant, 92. *See also* Old
   Covenant.
Moses, 29, 64, 96, 111
Mysticism, 82-83, 113
Nabataean desert, 37
Nazarenes, 18
Nazareth, 3, 13-14, 16, 23, 27, 35,
   133

Nehemiah, 11
Nero Caesar, 128
New American Bible, 98, 106
New Covenant, 92-93, 96-97, 121
New Israel, 29, 121-122, 127
New Jerusalem, 129
New Moses, 29
Nicodemus, 109
Numbers, 29
Numerology, 128
Old Covenant, 97, 121. *See also*
    Mosaic Covenant.
Old Jerusalem, 129
Old Testament, 1, 15, 28-29, 32, 55,
    60, 62, 64, 75, 94, 107,
    119-122
Onesimus, 78
Palestine, 2, 12, 29, 39, 75, 81, 91,
    102
Parables of Jesus
    Lost Sheep, the, 31
    Prodigal Son, the, 31
    Silver Piece, the, 31
Parousia, the, 42-43, 45, 62-63. *See
    also* the Day of the Lord, the
    Endtime, the End times, the
    Final Coming, the Last Day,
    the Last Judgment, the Second
    Coming.
Pastoral Letters, the, 70, 71-73,
    75-77, 83. *See also 1 and 2
    Timothy, Titus.*
Patmos, 117-118
Paul, 8-9, 14-15, 17-19, 27, 39-44,
    51-54, 56-57, 59, 63, 69, 71-
    72, 75, 78, 82-84, 87-88, 91
Pentecost, 17
People of the Book, 1, 15, 94, 120
People of the Way, 133
Pessinus, 57
Peter, 17-18, 25, 27, 34-35, 40, 57,
    75, 77, 104
1 Peter, 4, 8-9, 69, 76-77
2 Peter, 4, 69, 77-78
Peter's Profession of Faith, 25, 34-35
Petra, 37
Pharaoh, 127
Philemon, 40, 78
Philemon, 4, 8-9, 69, 78
Philip, 18

Philippi, 40, 44, 53-54
Philippians, 40, 53-54
Philippians, 4, 8-9, 51-55, 58, 66
Philo, 92
Plato, 92
Platonism, 92, 95. *See also* Greek
    philosophy, Hellenistic
    philosophy.
Pontus, 49
Porcius Festus, 71
Presbyters, 72-73
Proclamation, 1, 2, 4, 14, 19, 25. *See
    also* Kerygma.
Prologue, the (*John*), 106, 115
Prophetic writing, 120
Proto-Matthew, 25-26
Q (Quelle), 26
Rabbinical argumentation, 91, 96-97
Reconciliation, 61-63
Redemption, 61-63, 89, 95
Resurrection, 4, 15, 25, 55, 60-63,
    66, 75
Revelation, 5, 8-9, 60, 117-129, 131.
    See also the Apocalypse.
Revelatory writing, 120
Romans, 12, 40, 59, 91, 103,
    117-119
Romans, 4, 8-9, 51-52, 55, 58-67, 87
Rome, 40, 59, 71, 78, 82-84, 91,
    118, 128-129
Sacraments, the, 112-113
Salvation, 59, 61, 63, 78, 93, 119,
    124
Second Coming, the, 42, 77. *See also*
    the Day of the Lord, the
    Endtime, the End times, the
    Final Coming, the Last Day,
    the Last Judgment, the
    Parousia.
Second stage of New Testament
    development, the, 4, 5, 19,
    24, 28, 31, 35, 41, 43, 48, 52,
    58-60, 64, 69-70, 78-79, 98.
    See also Intimacy.
Seven Churches, the, 126
Seven seals, the, 126-127
Silas, 41
Simon, 74
Sin, 61-62, 64, 114
Sinful Woman, the, 31

Stage One. *See* the First stage of New
    Testament development,
    Infatuation.
Stage Three. *See* the Third stage of
    New Testament development,
    Identification.
Stage Two. *See* the Second stage of
    New Testament development,
    Intimacy.
Stephen, 18
Suffering servant, 12, 28, 35
Symbols in *Revelation*, 122-123
Synagogue, 13, 50, 75
Synoptic Gospels, the, 24-27, 31, 35,
    40-42, 47, 74, 98, 103-107,
    109. *See also Matthew, Mark,
    Luke.*
Tarsus, 39
Tavium, 57
Temple, 11, 13, 94
Ten Commandments, 64
Teresa of Avila, 82, 113
Thessalonians, 40, 45
1 Thessalonians, 4, 8-9, 14, 41-43,
    83
2 Thessalonians, 4, 8-9, 41-43
Thessalonica, 40-41
Third stage of New Testament
    development, the, 5, 78-79,
    83, 89-90, 94-95, 101, 112-
    113. *See also* Identification.
Time, 77, 93-94. *See also
    Chronos, Kairos.*
Timothy, 41, 54, 72
1 Timothy, 4, 8-9, 69-73. *See also* the
    Pastoral Letters.
2 Timothy, 4, 8-9, 69-73. *See also* the
    Pastoral Letters.
Titus, 44, 72
Titus, 4, 8-9, 69-73. *See also* the
    Pastoral Letters.
Tobit, 11
Troas, 53
Twelve, the, 103-104, 109. *See also*
    Apostle(s).
Yahweh, 11, 12, 14, 32, 38, 62, 81,
    107, 109-110
Zacchaeus, 31
Zechariah, 120